TEMPLES OF CONSCIOUSNESS

Ascended Master Teachings of the Golden Cities

ALSO BY LORI TOYE

A Teacher Appears

Sisters of the Flame

Fields of Light

The Ever Present Now

New World Wisdom Series

I AM America Atlas

Points of Perception

Light of Awakening

Divine Destiny

Sacred Energies

Building the Seamless Garment

Freedom Star Book

I AM America Map

Freedom Star Map

6-Map Scenario

US Golden City Map

Temples of Consciousness

Ascended Master Teachings of the Golden Cities

GOLDEN CITY SERIES
BOOK FIVE

Lori Adaile Toye

I AM AMERICA PUBLISHING & DISTRIBUTING
P.O. Box 2511, Payson, Arizona, 85547, USA.
www.iamamerica.com

© (Copyright) 2019 by Lori Adaile Toye. All rights reserved. ISBN: 978-1-880050-27-9. All rights exclusively reserved, including under the Berne Convention and the Universal Copyright Convention. No part of this book may be reproduced or translated in any language or utilized in any form or by any means, electronic or mechanical, including photocopying, recording, or by any information storage and retrieval system, without written permission from the publisher. Published in 2019 by I AM America Seventh Ray Publishing International, P.O. Box 2511, Payson, Arizona, 85547, United States of America.

I AM America Maps and Books have been marketed since 1989 by I AM America Seventh Ray Publishing and Distributing, through workshops, conferences, and numerous bookstores in the United States and internationally. If you are interested in obtaining information on available releases please write or call:
I AM America, P.O. Box 2511, Payson, Arizona, 85547, USA. (928) 978-6435, or visit:
www.iamamerica.com
www.loritoye.com

Graphic Design and Typography by Lori Toye
Host and Questions by Lenard Toye
Editing by Elaine Cardall and Betsy Robinson

Love, in service, breathes the breath for all!

Print On Demand Version
10 9 8 7 6 5 4 3 2 1

"If humanity experiences tumultuous change, these areas preserve and protect the higher spiritual truths.

If humanity listens to the prophets, these areas evolve and align humanity with the light."

~ Saint Germain

Contents

FOREWORD *by Barbara Moffitt* xix
PREFACE xxiii

CHAPTER ONE
Path of Light • 27

Sacrifice and the Unfolding 27
The Journey into Light........................... 28
Self-Judgment and the Web of Illusion 28
The Light within Overcomes Darkness and Duality 29
Trinity Is Union 30
The Lords of Venus and the Violet Flame............. 31
The Inner Earth and the Violet Ray................. 31
Seven Temples Anchor the Violet Ray............... 32
Diet and Vibration................................ 32
The Secret Chamber Re-dedicates the
  Ray for Humanity 32
Release of Genetic Fear 33
You Are Never Alone 33
Violet Flame Decree to Transmute Genetic Fear 34
Learning through Polarity......................... 34
Eternal I AM Presence 35
Violet Flame for Attacks and Threats 36
The Violet Flame and the Golden Cities 37

CHAPTER TWO
Teachings on Vibration • 39

Acceleration of Light and Sound 39
Dietary Guidelines for Vibration 40
Addiction to Fear 40
Assimilation of Light and Sound through Diet 41
The Fear Substance and the Plant Kingdom. 41
The Mighty Tube of Light 42
Higher Refinement through the Violet Flame 43
The Connection Within. 43
El Morya's Meditation Technique 44
Contact with the Master 44
Mastery of Thoughts, Feelings, and Actions. 45
Sacrifice as Energy for Energy 46
A Decree to Break Addiction 46
A Sacred Write and Burn Technique 47
The Dominant Ray of the Astral Body 47
Call Forth the Ray to Action 48
The Master Teacher Assists the Chela 48
Unseen Energy 49
Compassion Heals the Emotional Body 50
Sympathetic Harmony and the Law of Attraction 50
Synergistic Success 51
The Animal Kingdom 52

CHAPTER THREE
Stars of the Golden Cities • 55

Momentum of the Violet Ray 55
Golden City Grid. 56
The Golden City Star: Eight Lei-lines 56

Alignment of the Will 57
"As Above, So Below" 57
Unite As One Heart 57
"I AM As ONE" 58
The Law of Cooperation 58
Five Teachings of Spiritual Acceleration 58
The Ascension Spiral 59
Appearance of the Masters 59
Growth through the Earth Changes 60
Transmuting Self-created Hells 60
The Consent of Babajeran 61
The Great Purification 61
Gift of Spiritual Freedom 62
Acceleration in the Stars 62
Akashic History of Humanity 63
The Great Mystery Schools 63
Golden City Network 64
Ray Forces and Star Seeds 65
Levels of Harmony 66
Spiritual Initiation and Collective Consciousness
   in the Golden City 66
Where We Go ONE, We Go All 67
The Ascension Valleys 67
Stars and Interconnectivity 68
Integration and the Four Doorways 69
Violet Flame Decree for the Golden City Journey 70

CHAPTER FOUR

Ascension of Consciousness • 71

Cause and Effect 71

Alignment and Harmony 72

"Love, in Action" 72

Healing and the Ascension 73

Spiritual Education 74

Karmic Patterns 74

"The Reward Is Immeasurable" 75

Review Your Patterns 75

The Heart and Sacred Fire 76

Beyond Illusion 76

Invoke the Flame 77

Taming Emotions 77

Growth through Experience 78

The Mighty I AM Presence 79

The Awakening Point 79

Beyond the Physical 80

The Ascension Process 81

Ascension and Diet 81

Divine Love 82

Action and the Violet Flame 83

Emotional Attachments 84

Energy for Energy 85

Emotions and the Violet Flame 85

CHAPTER FIVE
Temples of Consciousness • 87

The Path of Forgiveness 87
Collective Consciousness and Change. 88
Spiritual Function of the Golden Cities 88
Genetic Manipulation 90
Perfection of the Unfed Flame 90
Command the Flame. 91
Choice and the Will. 92
The Spoken Word 92
Healing through the Temples of Consciousness 93
Temple of Gobean 94
Temple of Malton 95
Temple of Wahanee 95
Temple of Shalahah. 96
Temple of Klehma 96
Evolution through the Perfect Cell 97
Chakras and the Five Golden Cities 98
Temples of Evolution and Light 99

CHAPTER SIX
True Memory • 101

Time and Illusion 101
Mind, Choice, Action, and Memory. 102
Inhibiting Perceptions of Self 103
Surrender Judgments. 104
Freedom through Love 105
Experience the God-Man. 105
The Pleasant Prison 106
Expansion through Experience .106

Bliss or Pain? 106
Interconnected 107
Memory, Choice, and Natural Selection 108
Detachment and Love 108
Oversoul 109
Beyond Illusion 110
Experience the True Self 110
Soul Knows All 111
Fountain of Youth 111
A Developed Memory 112
Forgiveness and Natural Law 112
Awakening 113
Compassion, Mercy, Freedom 113

CHAPTER SEVEN

Ascension through the Dimensions • 115

The Spiritual Training of the Mind 115
Ascension of Souls 116
The Open Heart 116
Preparation through the Golden Cities 117
Parallel and Paradox 117
A Unified Body of Light 118
The Unseen Kingdoms 118
Translation between the Dimensions 119
Life Beyond 119
Golden Cities and the Fourth Dimension 119
The Fourth Dimension and Earth Changes 120
An Exponential Leap 121
Energy Fields of the Fourth Dimension 122
A Range of Ray Forces 122
When the Time Is Right 123

Babajeran and the Elemental Life Force 124
The Divine Oneship of Nature 125
Opening the Divine Cell 125
Change and Choice 126
Interconnectivity 126
Sound Frequencies 127
Perception 127
Divine Chamber of the Heart 129
The Ascension Process and the Master Teacher 130

CHAPTER EIGHT
The Heart of Peace • 131

Making Sense Out of the Senseless 131
Time of Testing 132
Polarization and Diverse Experiences 133
The Master Leads through Universal Laws 134
The Calm of "Knowing" 134
Aggregate Body of Light 135
Violet Flame to Open Light 135
Violet Flame for Our World Leaders 136
"The Answer Is Not Simplistic" 137
Take Time, Wait, Observe, Watch 138
The Christ Within 138
When You Are Hindered by Fear 140
Moving Out of Darkness 140
The Golden City Star 142
The Silent Masters 143
Individualization Upon a Ray 143
Seven Points per Doorway 144
Golden City Retreats 144
The Master Appears 144

CHAPTER NINE
Unified Plane of Understanding • 147

During Times of Fear．．．．．．．．．．．．．．．．．．．．．．．．．．．147
Intention and Self-examination．．．．．．．．．．．．．．．．．．．148
Balancing the Dual Forces．．．．．．．．．．．．．．．．．．．．．．．149
Timeless, Breathless Energy．．．．．．．．．．．．．．．．．．．．．．150
"The Divine Plan Is Always Working"．．．．．．．．．．．．．．150
Beyond Death and Separation．．．．．．．．．．．．．．．．．．．．151
The Christ Plane．．．．．．．．．．．．．．．．．．．．．．．．．．．．．．．152
Use of Meditation．．．．．．．．．．．．．．．．．．．．．．．．．．．．．．153
Groups of Seven．．．．．．．．．．．．．．．．．．．．．．．．．．．．．．．．154
Protection in the Stars．．．．．．．．．．．．．．．．．．．．．．．．．．．155
Daily Practice for the Golden City Star．．．．．．．．．．．．．．155
Creating Harmony．．．．．．．．．．．．．．．．．．．．．．．．．．．．．．155
Spiritual Practice in the Golden City Doorways．．．．．．．156
Masters of the Heart．．．．．．．．．．．．．．．．．．．．．．．．．．．．．157
A Template in Place．．．．．．．．．．．．．．．．．．．．．．．．．．．．．157
Alchemy in Nature．．．．．．．．．．．．．．．．．．．．．．．．．．．．．．158
Teaching and Healing．．．．．．．．．．．．．．．．．．．．．．．．．．．．158
The Temple Divine．．．．．．．．．．．．．．．．．．．．．．．．．．．．．．159
Co-creation through Our Beliefs．．．．．．．．．．．．．．．．．．．161
The Master Lies Within．．．．．．．．．．．．．．．．．．．．．．．．．．161
Tolerance．．．．．．．．．．．．．．．．．．．．．．．．．．．．．．．．．．．．．．162

CHAPTER TEN
Principles of Harmony • 163

Acceptance of All．．．．．．．．．．．．．．．．．．．．．．．．．．．．．．．．163
Balance．．164
Calm．．164
Oneness．．．．．．．．．．．．．．．．．．．．．．．．．．．．．．．．．．．．．．．165

A Daily Practice for Harmony................................. 165
Harmony Vibrates at the Heart Chakra 167
Harmony Builds a Force Field............................. 168
Two Become As One 169
One Step at a Time 169
The Blue Flame of Harmony................................ 170
Expansion of Consciousness................................. 171
The Chaos before Balance................................... 171
"Harmony Is a Level of Conscious Activity" 173
Group Harmony 173
Karma and Use of the Violet Flame 175
Service and the Release of Karma 175
Sananda's Peace Meditation 177

CHAPTER ELEVEN
Science of Solution • 179

Awakening and Moving beyond Fear 179
The Perfected State of the I AM Presence 180
Love, Joy, and the Master Within 181
Moving through Crisis... 182
Solving Problems through the ONE..................... 183
Polarity Births Neutrality..................................... 184
Removing Problematic Blocks with the Violet Flame ... 184
Problems, Choice, and Solutions 185
Empowerment through God I AM 186
Prophecy and Positive Energy............................. 186
Awakening the Divinity Within 187
Effect of Higher Consciousness........................... 188
Twelve, a Sacred Number of Expansion 189
The Two Suns.. 190

Release of Negative Turmoil 190
Golden City Star Mudra 191

Appendix A: *The Three Standards* — 195
Appendix B: *Candle Meditation* — 197
Appendix C: *Write and Burn Technique* — 199
Appendix D: *The Great Purification* — 201
Appendix E: *Chakras and the Five United States Golden Cities* — 203
Appendix F: *Seven Adjutant Points of a Golden City Doorway* — 205
Appendix G: *Sunday Peace Meditation* — 207
Spiritual Lineage of the Violet Flame — 211
Glossary — 213
Discography — 231
Index — 233
About Lori & Lenard Toye — 247
About I AM America — 250

Foreword

Over the last three years it has been my pleasure to study the I AM America mystery school teachings with Lori Toye. Back in 2015, I was browsing the I AM America website and saw that Lori offered weekly classes via phone conference calls. I contacted the website, and, as of today, our study group has covered eleven books in a series of channeled materials received by Lori from the Ascended Masters. *Temples of Consciousness,* is the fifth book in the series of seven books about the Golden City information released through Saint Germain and other Ascended Teachers of the Spiritual Hierarchy.

The Great Awakening is upon us! We are in the Time of Change-now. I was told in a meditation more than six years ago, "It is the dividing time." As a teacher and spiritual seeker, I'd concluded that the physical laws that rule our universe must mirror the spiritual laws that govern our participation in it. So I was always trying to find the laws that governed life and death, my plan for being here, and the book that had a simple list that could guide me. My husband and I joined an Association for Research and Enlightnment study group back in the 1970s to review the Edgar Cayce materials. This opened my journey into spirituality, the soul, Earth Changes, karma, Ascension, and the path of spiritual enlightenment. We joined a meditation group that focused on our dreams and awakening the inner life. My spirit guides led each step, "Read this book . . . go there . . . meet this person."

My new Awakening brought me to the Unity Movement. A new Unity church in my hometown opened a Montessori School. I knew a bit about Maria Montessori so I went to investigate the school for my two young children. I enrolled them, but first I had to be sure what principles the Unity church espoused. Well, here I found the simple spiritual laws that govern life-you create your experience by your own thoughts, feelings, and actions. Through this way of life, you are in charge of your own happiness. I was quickly promoted from a volunteer to the director of the new Montessori School. So off I went to study Montessori philosophy and the education of young children.

Montessori philosophy states that each child is a spiritual being, to be treated with dignity and respect, to be listened to, and guided gently in a prepared learning environment. Right up my alley! This harmonized with my professional and personal beliefs. My role in this movement was to span forty-five years and I opened accredited Montessori schools, trained teachers, led national organizations, and published Montessori materials. Also, I led state and national conferences and created teacher training centers throughout North America and Central and South America,

During this time my list of spiritual studies and their spiritual laws grew longer and longer. More questions? Find the answer! My understanding of the necessary spiritual qualities and their development became clear. New doors and windows opened. I am a person who needs to see how a spiritual law demonstrates itself and if it is really the Truth. All these lessons brought me to the *I AM America* materials which summarize the great spiritual teachings. The Ascended Master teachings give the roadmap to understand the language of light and sound, and how it manifests into the Divine Self.

The Montessori philosophy follows a simple cosmic principle: initiate, practice, apply. It is up to each one of us to follow this if we want to find the Divine Temple within. *Temples of Consciousness* describes the spiritual practices to find our inner divinity. To walk in the garden with God requires focus, discipline, meditation, prayers, decrees, and mantras, use of the Violet Flame, visualization, breath work, proper diet, and intention. In so doing, you raise your vibration and frequency. Light and sound move us through the Eight-sided Cell of Perfection and its pathway of love, mercy, compassion, and forgiveness. The faults we see in others are the faults we see in ourselves. As we move deeper, our energy fields clear to reveal our illusions and to face our personal fears. We untie the cords that bind us, release our faulty thinking, and come back to our Divine Holy Temple. Transmutation and healing begin. We are never alone, and we are never separated from the Divine.

The Ascended Masters have co-created a new energy grid around our planet. There are now 51 Golden City Vortices spread throughout the Earth. The five Golden Cities located in the United States are fully active. These centers are safe places where light and sound are magnified and intensified. You can live in a Golden City or visit them. These geographic centers aid your alchemical transformation into higher consciousness and understanding of the physical self, the immortal soul, and the divinity within. The Golden Cities have been given to us as a Divine Intervention so we can focus on our own self-mastery. The Ascended Masters have promised to teach in these temples about our spiritual heritage. Freedom is our birthright.

As you read *Temples of Consciousness*, may your soul be touched, whereby you see your Divine Plan, find your path to liberation, and walk daily with your I AM Presence. As each soul moves forward, it benefits the whole planet. "Where we go one, we go all," is the inscription written on the bell of J. F. K.'s yacht. *Temples of Consciousness* will awaken you to the cosmic laws of the great Divine Plan and the interconnectedness of life. You will find the blueprint to perfection which results in peace, prosperity, and joy for yourself and all the brothers and sisters who wish to follow. The great spiritual laws we have been given can be summarized in two simple statements:

> "You shall love the Lord, your God, with all your heart, with all your soul and with all your mind, and you shall love your neighbor as yourself."
> Matthew 22: 37-39

We are all here to initiate the Golden Age. It is NOW!

Barbara Moffitt

Barbara has been a teacher all her life, having graduated from the University of Missouri with a BS in Education. Furthering her studies, she gained a Specialist Certification in Language and Learning Disabilities. She later earned a Master's Degree in Metaphysics from Delphi University in NW Georgia. She studied Montessori Education throughout the US and is a certified Early Childhood Montessori Educator and Trainer. She was a founding member of the National Center for Montessori Education and the Montessori Accreditation Council for Teacher Education, later joining the American Montessori Society. She and her husband owned and operated private schools for ages two through twelve in Texas and Georgia, along with the Atlanta Montessori Teacher Education Center in Atlanta, Georgia, for forty years.

Barbara is now retired and lives in North Carolina in the foothills of the Appalachian Mountains. Having spent her life in the Midwest, Texas, and Georgia, she now enjoys a quieter life living by the lake, caring for the birds and flowers and, of course, still reading and learning. She and her husband organized a new spiritual home nearby where they volunteer their time in service. They also started a spiritual meditation retreat Airbnb in North Georgia. They love traveling, visiting their two children, two granddaughters, and two great grandchildren. Life is good.

Preface

In this fifth book in the *Golden City Series*, we continue our journey with the Ascended Masters, learning/studying their teachings of the divine intervention that empowers worldwide Golden Cities. These metaphysical havens aid humanity's spiritual evolution and destined result—Ascension. While perusing this new manuscript, I found a unique passage. (See this book's first pages.) Saint Germain, the primary teacher of the *I AM America* material, is uncertain if human beings will indeed make the evolutionary passage from human to the Ascended state. Our survival may be through the enduring energies of the Golden Cites that persevere alongside the ongoing and tumultuous Earth Changes that ravage our planet. He prophesies the Golden Cities protect essential spiritual energies that nurture humanity's latent, innate, and divine heritage. However, alternatively, he prophesies an optimistic evolution for humanity through the birth of the New Times with our entrance into the consciousness-calibrating energies of the Golden Age.

At a one-dimensional viewpoint, it's a bit of a no-brainer: I want a Golden Age and all the goodies that come with it for embodied human beings. Unfortunately, there seem to be many steps in between the first whiff of self-conscious awareness and living in a state of spiritual liberation. The Masters call the remarkable journey between these steps the "Ascension Process"—a process that contains numerous levels of noteworthy spiritual passages that awaken, shock, confirm, align, and inevitably empower the human to HUman evolution. In the *I AM America Trilogy*, the Spiritual Teachers refer to this personal development as the *Spiritual Awakening*. Today, humanity's initiation magnifies and stirs emotions throughout the world, righteously illuminating dark, hidden corners as government and secret program insiders spill covert knowledge to seek redemption and light. Citizen journalists refer to this time as the *Great Awakening*. No coincidence that Golden Cities have been active since 1984.

Perhaps the Great Ones who over-light our Earth with spiritual wisdom and protection knew all along of the strategic and clandestine evil designed to literally keep humanity in the dark. So the Masters communicated their higher knowledge in a simplistic way so we could understand. This effort produced the *I AM America Maps*: prophecies of massive earthquakes, volcanic eruptions, global warming, and melting of the polar-caps, alongside civil unrest and social turbulence. What if they had said HAARP creates earthquakes or Chemtrails obscure vital galactic light? Or weather modification can create huge global superstorms that span hundreds of miles? I'm certain we would have dismissed these facts as wacky conspiracy and never recognized or accepted our precarious and dangerous situation. I still remember watching the trajectory of Hurricane Irma in 2017 and its astonishing size—covering the *entire* peninsula state of Florida.

The Spiritual Masters took the high road. Instead of reveling in this almost incomprehensible evil or reverting to apocalyptic porn, they simply reminded us of who we were and what we had forgotten. They simply stated: You are divinely engendered Co-creators. And they reiterated, "This is who you are eternally. This is your Divine Inheritance." Plus, their advice is infused with numerous techniques and spiritual practices designed to cultivate our innate divinity and to achieve our victory in the light. Yes, this is the true plan. We are to be free.

Where does one start? Obviously, with this book or any other *I AM America* publication. The lessons in these pages walk you through the release of genetically held fear and teach us how every negative situation we encounter is an opportunity to learn through polarity. Also included are suggestions to attune our diet and break negative addictions while cultivating compassion, especially for self. And that's just the first two chapters! Since this information was received both pre- and post 9-11, the Masters' instruction reads like the contents from a poetic time bottle: "This is what you do before the SHTF (Sh*t Hits the Fan) . . . and, this is what you do after."

Immediately post-9-11, we were instructed to light candles and to pray, and increase our spiritual practice in the Stars, the powerful centers of the Golden Cities. And through some miracle, our collective pleas to the heavens were answered by the great ones—the Divine Beings, the Mighty Archangels and Elohim, the Cosmic and Galactic Masters, and the Great White Brotherhood. A clarion call sounded and thousands of light beings flooded the Golden Cities to establish Fourth and Fifth Dimensional Ashrams of Light at specific power points. This is where humanity's spiritual development could initiate the Golden Age, through the gentle, yet wise, Earth Mother,

Babajeran, alongside our brothers and sisters of expanded light in wondrous *Temples of Consciousness*.

I invite you to read and practice the spiritual advice and techniques described in these pages. You will learn how to expand your super senses and to identify and feel subtle, heavenly energy. Then travel to a Golden City and enter one of its magnificent doorways. Allow the energies of an adjutant point to caress your spirit, and journey onward, into the sanction of its luminous Star. Claim your freedom and innate HU-man divinity. This is the glorious beginning of your victorious Ascension Process.

> "Mighty Violet Ray stream forth from the Fifth Dimension
> into the hearts of men.
> May the Fourth Dimension bring its alignment
> for greater purification of the Earth Divine.
> May all align and Ascend in thy flame."
>
> *Lori Toye*

1

Path of Light
Saint Germain

Greetings Beloved chelas in that mighty Violet Ray. I AM Saint Germain and I stream forth on that Violet Ray of Mercy, Compassion, and Forgiveness. As usual Dear hearts, I request permission to come forward.

Response: *Please Saint Germain, come forward.*

SACRIFICE AND THE UNFOLDING

There is much within your mind this morning, is there not Dear ones, Dear hearts? For you see, the work that you have been given to do, you now understand at another level. You understand the sacrifice that is necessary to continue upon this path. You understand now the great sacrifice of the adepts and the avatars. You understand the true unfolding of the rose eternal and the meaning of that within. Realize Dear hearts, Dear chelas of mine, that the Unfed Flame of Love, Wisdom, and Power is always within you, guiding and directing you. It is this Flame of Divinity that we serve. It is this Flame that exists within the heart of humanity, that serves that greater cause and brings humanity into its greater and whole revolution.

THE JOURNEY INTO LIGHT

Dear ones, Dear hearts, realize also that the soul, in its sojourn in this physical world of learning about thought, feeling, and action has many activities that are brought forward for a greater refinement and into a greater knowledge. Understand that these are only lessons. They are not who you are or what you are. The lessons are only the experiences that will lead you onward and upward in your evolution into this journey of light. The journey of light is indeed one where one must understand and face the negative force, the dark side of their own being. They must accept then and understand all that has existed within them, those things that they judge and have not accepted. The harshest of all judgment always comes from the judgment of self, does it not?

Answer: *Yes.*

SELF-JUDGMENT AND THE WEB OF ILLUSION

Working with every meet and measure, the individual, in the experience of the soul's journey, comes forward in a more regal expression and judges each experience, saying, "I am imperfect. I did not do the best that I could do." But do not let this be the end result of what you do Dear ones, Dear hearts. Understand that all is given for a greater timing and intention. Understand that each experience is woven into that seamless garment. Then and only then, as each experience is put together and woven into that finer cloth of understanding, is one able to stand firm and free. It is only through the use of this mighty Violet Ray that you are freed from these creations of the mind, freed of these creations of self-judgment.

How does one know when they are engaging in these acts of self-judgment? When they judge others. For you see Dear one, Dear heart, when one finds fault within another, they are faults that they see within themselves. These are the little stumbling blocks that the individual, in the process of understanding the soul, encounters on the path of light. Onward and upward we tread this path, looking for the source eternal...looking for the answers to the questions... looking for that perfect goal and mind. Understand, as it has always been said unto you, "that perfection lies within. That all divinity is within."

May the Violet Ray stream forth into the hearts of humanity.
    May perfection reign supreme, for it is as it is,
        I AM THAT I AM.

THE LIGHT WITHIN OVERCOMES DARKNESS AND DUALITY

Within this grand and mighty statement, is a statement of perfection. Perfection exists within and is ever evolving and ever expressing itself. The false, or the dark side of the being, we must face or let go as an illusion. You see Dear ones, Dear hearts, in this web of illusion, created to educate you to the quality and integrity of your choice, at times you begin to accept that the illusion has more strength than that mighty Light of God that Never, Never Faileth. Know Dear ones, Dear hearts, that light dwells within you and it is the intention of the Great White Brotherhood and Sisterhood of Light to fan that flame ever eternal within you. It is that flame that holds the mighty key, not only of your evolution, but of your Oneship and connection to Unana.

Brothers and Sisters of light, unite unto the ONE. Understand this mighty flame in action within you. Understand, when you accept this light eternal, there are no mistakes, ever, ever, ever. The randomness you would judge as stupidity, or judge as a mistake, or you would judge simply to judge does not exist. Know that all things fit into that plan eternal. Know that all things are connected unto this ONE. There is a grand web of life; join unto it Dear ones, Dear hearts. Enter into that mighty Breath of God that Never, Never Faileth.

When one faces and understands the illusions and fears that exist within, they are being prepared and readied for another course of Divine Action. The actions upon the Earth Plane and Planet are the stored karmas of what you have encountered within another lifetime. But these actions also serve the next lifetime; for eventually, through each of these actions, you are brought to a greater understanding and quality on the path of light. Dear ones, Dear hearts, understand that in this field of action, that indeed there is turmoil, pitfalls, and great nights of darkness but these are perceived only through limitation. Know this: in the darkest moment is also that mighty Light of God that is shining within it all, weaving it together into that seamless garment, that mighty cloth of experience. It is important to have experience, is it not? For then one understands the limitation of duality. Yes, Dear chelas of mine, the dual experience is indeed limited.

TRINITY IS UNION

When one enters into that pure light of the Christ Consciousness, one then understands the trinity that is born out of the union of the two. Where all forces meet as ONE, light and darkness become ONE. Mother and father become ONE, united with the child. It is this simple Dear ones, Dear hearts, and yet when one is still trapped in the chains of illusion, it is difficult to see that there is another way. There is another perception through the uncluttering of the mind and through the use of that mighty Violet Ray. You then are able to see where the door will open and that light of hope enters into the experience. It is important to understand that this is why we have brought the work of that mighty Violet Ray. I would like to bring to you now a brief history concerning the Violet Ray, so you will understand it in its entirety and complexity at times. It is a very, very simple law in motion.

THE LORDS OF VENUS AND THE VIOLET FLAME

The Violet Ray is a law eternal of this solar system. It was brought by the Lords of Venus to end the suffering of the minds of men and create a clean slate, so all may be brought to a greater and a higher understanding. In the beginning, this mighty Violet Ray was a frequency of sound. It was held within the electromagnetic field of the Lords of Venus when they came to Earth to bring forward a greater harmony and a greater knowledge for those who were suffering. It had been deemed by the great force above that this mighty ray, this sound vibration, would be brought for the healing of the masses. Not only would it be brought forward as a sound ray, as it was developed in its earlier form, but it was also brought forth as a light ray. There are even beings who incarnate upon this light and sound ray, to hold the focus for one lifetime upon the eternal healing and balance among humanity.

THE INNER EARTH AND THE VIOLET RAY

The Violet Ray was anchored in seven locations throughout the planet. In the beginning, these were held within the Earth itself, in secret locations where it was allowed to vibrate through the vibral core of the poles of the Earth. In the days of Atlantis, the vibration increased into its higher form. This would be, not the end time of Atlantis, but the earlier years of the formation of this culture. This was a time that you would call the ending of a Silver Age, before consciousness fell into the Bronze Age. This mighty Violet Ray was then brought to the surface of the Earth and celebrated and held in traditions within the mighty temples.

SEVEN TEMPLES ANCHOR THE VIOLET RAY

Seven temples were built strategically on the locations where this mighty Violet Ray was held. These locations are not pertinent now in this teaching, but you shall understand that they too existed where eight lei-lines were intersecting. The Earth and these eight lei-lines brought that Violet Ray forward for those who would invoke its use. The Violet Ray was then anchored, not only in the Earth and in those mighty Lords of Venus who came, but through the process of initiation with sound vibration, in the chelas who took up this study of Mercy, Compassion, and Forgiveness.

DIET AND VIBRATION

Strict guidelines were given regarding the diet. These of course were given to alter the vibration and, as you well know, once the vibration is altered, the physical body then follows. Children of a higher vibration were then birthed and brought forth in this great evolution of the Violet Ray. But then there is always a choice, is there not Dear ones, Dear hearts? There were those who came among humanity whose consciousness fell off again into genetic manipulation and the eating of flesh and the consciousness fell into a state of muck and mire.

THE SECRET CHAMBER RE-DEDICATES THE RAY FOR HUMANITY

Now, as I have stated earlier in this discourse, there is never, ever a random act and this allowed for a greater understanding of the importance of this mighty ray. It was taken back into the secret chambers of the Earth and there it stayed until a time, within the early part of this century, (twentieth century), when it was allowed to be taught again to those whose eyes, ears, and hearts were opened. This mighty Ray in action combines all forces of all mantras that have existed to help and assist mankind. Calling upon it calls for a unity within the self. Calling upon it creates the release from the bondage of time and its illusions.

RELEASE OF GENETIC FEAR

There is much, much more to the science of this mighty ray. There is much, much more in understanding its application. But know this Dear ones, Dear hearts, when you call upon this mighty Violet Ray of Mercy, Compassion, and Forgiveness, you call upon those who have gone before you…you call upon those who use it in the heavens eternal…you call upon those who have anchored it firmly within the core of beloved Babajeran…you call forth Divine Intervention to solve any problem, any mistake, any judgment of self. The judgments of self are perhaps the hardest to overcome and understanding the web of illusion. For you to address that great fear that is held genetically within the cells, that fear that you are working to bring a great release to, that mighty Violet Ray prepares you to put that Law of Love into action…it prepares you for the higher consciousness…it prepares you for the birth of the Christ eternal.

YOU ARE NEVER ALONE

Know this Dear ones, Dear hearts, that when you call upon this mighty flame in action, anchored within your heart, it brings a vibration that emanates throughout your whole electromagnetic pulse. It then anchors itself to the central core of the Earth and onward to the Great Central Sun. Know that when you call upon that mighty Violet Ray in action, that there are thousands and thousands and thousands joining you in that instant and moment. Know that you are never alone in what you do. Know that you are connected to a higher purpose, to a higher journey on the path of light. I shall now open the floor for questions.

VIOLET FLAME DECREE TO TRANSMUTE GENETIC FEAR

Question: *Yes, thank you. Is there a specific Violet Flame Decree that can be brought forth for the transmutation of all that genetically held fear?*

Mighty Violet Ray, stream forth from the Mighty Logos of
the Great Central Sun.
Anchor the Rays of Transmutation, Forgiveness, and Compassion within my heart. May this Violet Ray now emanate
throughout my being.
May this Violet Ray serve the Cause Divine.

Mighty Violet Ray, come forth in the emanation of the
Christ.
Mighty Violet Ray, come forth in the emanation of I AM
THAT I AM.
Mighty Violet Ray, serve all those who come forward to serve
a Cause Divine.
Align the great heart of compassion and the great will of the
Divine Order
to come forth in Cause Divine.

Mighty Violet Ray, I AM THAT I AM.
Mighty Violet Ray, I AM the beginning, I AM the end.
Mighty Violet Ray, I AM the Alpha, the Omega.
Mighty Violet Ray, SO BE IT! IT IS DONE.

LEARNING THROUGH POLARITY

Question: *Thank you. In the beginning of this discourse, you talked about how light and dark are joined as the mother and father are joined. Are you saying, for all of humanity, that these opposing forces become joined in that evolutionary process?*

It is so Dear ones, Dear hearts, for how could you ever sense heat without sensing cold? And there, you are able to distinguish one from the other. Of course, when you begin to study hermetic law, you can take this understanding of duality to many things: to the cycles of rhythm, as you see in the sun and the moon; to polarization, that exists between those of one light field to a next. I have explained this concept through the principle of sympathetic resonance. Duality brings a myriad of great teaching but remember, it is indeed a web only given for understanding. It is important to invoke that mighty Violet Ray and the decree that I have just given you, to raise the consciousness into a higher understanding, into a higher knowledge of how all forces work together for that great and mighty ONE. There is one force guiding and directing all things. Know and understand this and you will have a greater supreme knowledge.

ETERNAL I AM PRESENCE

Question: *Thank you. As we have discussed before, humanity's evolution is assured, so am I to understand in this discourse, that the purpose of illusion and its education through duality has completed it mission?*

For those who are readied and have the eyes to see and the ears to hear, it is complete and leads one to a greater knowing that peace reigns supreme. But yet, there are always those who remain, who have not captured that essence of unity and still feel separation within their being...still feel that they are no longer tied to the great Divine Plan...feel, as you would say, hung out to dry. But these feelings of separation, know that they are illusion. Know that all is interconnected with the greater Plan Divine. Know that the mighty I AM Presence is serving you at all times and it is anchored within that great flame in the heart of your being. This is who you are eternally. This is your Divine Inheritance.

We are united as ONE…we are united in a greater plan…we are as ONE. As Dear Sananda has said, "Om Sheahah, I AM as ONE." This is the greater understanding of the dyad. It is the greater understanding which moves one into the trinity. The great sacrifice of the adepts and the Avatars is the sacrificing of the ego and the letting down of all fear. By letting down the little traps, they move into that greater reality and the understanding of the ONE. This is a new consciousness, yes, for many but know that I AM there. Know that, through the I AM THAT I AM, you are never alone, Dear ones, Dear hearts. You are always with the great Source of the ONE eternal. This mighty consciousness exists to serve all…this mighty consciousness exists to serve all circumstances…this mighty consciousness exists to serve all situations. Know and understand that it exists in all things. As you move out of judgment of others, you move out of judgment of self. You then begin to accept the divinity that lies within you. You then begin to pulse with the great Divine Flame that exists within you. Questions?

VIOLET FLAME FOR ATTACKS AND THREATS

Question: *Yes, in applying this on a day-to-day basis, if we have gotten insulting or attacking mail or messages, how would you suggest that we deal with those things?*

As you know, Dear one, Dear heart, in the Laws of Co-creation, these are but mirrors are they not, for you to gain a greater understanding of the work you are doing yourself? But shall we say, at the simplest level, bless all who come to attack; bless all who come to threaten. Understand that it is only there to mirror back the Law of ONE, to mirror back that mighty law in action that all will serve the law eternal. Know this and there you shall be free.

Question: *I see. So once again, is there a decree that we can utilize for such activities?*

Violet Flame purify. Violet Flame sanctify.
Violet Flame bring forth balance in this situation.
Violet Flame seal in love, Violet Flame eternal dove.
Violet Flame I AM, I AM, I AM.

THE VIOLET FLAME AND THE GOLDEN CITIES

Question: *Thank you. The Golden Cities, as they are activated, are they the power points of consciousness that then transmute?*

Not only do the Golden Cities channel the Ray Forces and qualify them for their highest use, as we have given you in other discourses, but the Violet Flame that resides within the inner Earth, anchored throughout both the North and the South Pole, filtrates up through that mighty vortex of power. The Violet Flame brings forward a greater healing of humanity at a mind level and from there, the emotions and the body. Then actions come forth.

Question: *I see. So the Golden Cities are a focus to bring complete balance of all of the Rays?*

They are the new temples that are now built, to bring about a greater understanding of the law eternal. As you see Dear ones, Dear hearts, is this not always as it is? One wave of souls incarnate upon the Earth Plane and Planet and then make their exit after they bring completion and understanding of their lessons. Then a new wave comes in. These great temples are designed to serve in their timing and intention for those who are readied to serve the Plan Divine.

Question: *I see. So the Golden Cities are temples where souls now go to become free?*

It is so Dear one, Dear heart and there will be those, if they come and have not cleared out their intention, that will be met by the law eternal and the Sacred Fire of the Violet Flame. Did you not note, when you moved into that Golden City of Gobean, that the first thing that you encountered were feelings of great disharmony, great discomfort? For you see, you were working to bring that Ray Force into a greater assimilation and integration. These are the law eternal. Now, those who are ready to serve the Cause Divine will assimilate these Ray Forces, will assimilate the Violet Ray through the new temples as they are built. But those who are not ready will simply turn their back and return to the world of illusion. Know that this is the law in its greater working, in its greater understanding. These higher subtle energy forces are not for those who are not readied. They are only for those who are readied. Do you understand?

Question: *Yes I do. So, are you also saying, that even those who might have the intention to stop or slow down the Golden City activation, that this is not possible?*

Dear one, Dear heart, as you know, when you invoke that mighty Violet Ray and bring it forth into your being, how can you stop the high frequency pitch? How can you stop the process of transmutation? How can you stop the feeling of love and joy in your heart? Questions?

Response: *That is very true. You can not stop it. Once you have stepped upon that wave, it carries you.*

And now Dear heart, unless, if you have further questions, I shall take my leave.

Response: *I thank you very much.*

2

Teachings On Vibration
Saint Germain

Greetings Beloved chelas in that mighty Christ. I AM Saint Germain and I stream forth on that Violet Ray of Mercy, Compassion, and ultimate Forgiveness. As usual Dear chelas, I ask permission to come forward.

Response: *Please Saint Germain, come forward. You are most welcome.*

ACCELERATION OF LIGHT AND SOUND

There is much work for us to complete. For you see Dear ones, Dear hearts, each discourse comes forward with a timing and intent. We bring forward this information to bring upliftment to those who have the eyes to see and the ears to hear. This information comes forward, not only to bring a continuity to this work, but to bring you to a higher understanding of your spiritual development and ultimate liberation in the Ascension of light and sound.

Light and sound is indeed the matrix, is it not, of the physical dimension of the Earth Plane and Planet? Through light and sound, all comes forward in its glory and intention of creation. Light and sound were at the beginning of the creation of this world, this Earthly schoolroom, so to speak, and light and sound bring its completion as you enter into that path of Ascension. It is indeed an acceleration of this vibration of light and sound, an acceleration that brings forward a greater rate of spin in the human aura itself. We have discussed this in prior discourses but you must understand

Dear ones, Dear hearts, that there are many other things that help to bring a greater adjustment and refinement to the energy fields of the human aura.

DIETARY GUIDELINES FOR VIBRATION

This great acceleration is of course affected by diet, for when you take an energy substance, a foodstuff, into yourself, are you not then placing that energy frequency and vibration into your being? That is why one of the beginning dietary guidelines for those who wish to bring this greater acceleration is to limit the intake of animal products. For you see Dear ones, Dear hearts, the vibration of this brings into the body a lower vibration. This lower vibration holds the body to the Earth Plane and Planet. As this body is held to the Earth Plane and Planet, the spirit wishes, in its ascent, to rise higher but it is limited by the flesh.

There are those who will say, "Isn't what comes from my mouth more important than what I put into my mouth?" It is most important what comes from your mind, Dear ones, Dear hearts. From that which you think, as we have always known, is that great and mighty builder of consciousness. But Dear ones, Dear hearts, to bring a greater discipline and refinement to the body, to bring it into higher vibration, it is important to understand to limit the intake of all fleshly products. This includes beef, chicken, fish, and seafoods of all varieties. You see Dear ones, Dear hearts, anything that has a nervous system attached to it, in terms of a Chakra System, when you remove that from the diet, you will see that you will have a greater refinement and a higher vibration to work within and without.

ADDICTION TO FEAR

These changes in the diet of course bring a greater acceleration to the body itself. It is also important to limit those foodstuffs that come from animals; these would be milk, eggs, and cheese products. For you see Dear ones, Dear hearts, again we are dealing with a vibration, are we not? Now I realize that your physiology is evolved or mutated to that point that it needs these types or substances of foods in order to bring forth its own sense of survival. This of course is an addiction to the fear substance itself. There have been those who have stated, "The reason that I do not eat flesh of any variety is because of its affiliation with fear through the death of the animal." It is true that some of this residue does remain after the death but it is also important to understand that we are dealing primarily again with light and sound frequencies and what is best for the body.

ASSIMILATION OF LIGHT AND SOUND THROUGH DIET

Now, to bring you to your higher evolution, I would ask that you limit the intake of these substances. One of the basic guidelines for the beginner is no less than three times per week but as you grow in your spiritual evolution and understanding, it is best to withdraw these to two times, one time, and then not at all within the diet. We realize that this will bring a greater disharmony in rescheduling and reworking your diet and your habits. But you see Dear ones, Dear hearts, by bringing this greater refinement and understanding to the system, it will indeed bring you into a higher vibration and into a greater assimilation of light and sound. There will be those chelas who will say with this request, "This is too difficult. This is too difficult for me to assimilate within my being and my body. And what of the vegetables and the fruit kingdoms, do they not go through a type of death?"

THE FEAR SUBSTANCE AND THE PLANT KINGDOM

It is important to understand Dear ones, Dear hearts, that when you use vegetables or fruits, that you are dealing with a different vibratory system altogether. The first thing to understand is that there are indeed emotions that are felt by plants and emotions that are felt throughout this mighty kingdom. But it is also important to understand that the fear substance does not penetrate the cell at the moment that it is used or harvested for human consumption. There is a higher refinement and a higher vibration that is brought forward. Of course, it is best then to eat the fruits, nuts, and vegetables that have already gone through their complete maturation process. That is why fruits and grains are the higher evolved dietary substances that you should use at this time. However, we realize that in your evolution and in the habits of your consciousness, that this may be difficult, so follow this standard guideline and it will bring you into a greater understanding of higher vibration and service to the Light of God that Never Fails.

THE MIGHTY TUBE OF LIGHT

Dear ones, Dear hearts, it is also important to always use that mighty Tube of Light. Now of course, I have always given you instruction in the use of the Violet Flame but it is important always, to keep that mighty Tube of Light surrounding you as well. This tube of pure white light keeps the connection always open to your mighty I AM Presence. This brings you into a greater integration of the Ray Forces from the Great Central Sun. The mighty I AM Presence acts as a step-down transformer of the Ray Forces. This mighty I AM Presence is the unseen force that acts as the transmitter of the Rays to the astral and light bodies and from there, light interacts throughout your energy fields. Putting this mighty Tube of Light on is very easy indeed. Call forth:

In the name of I AM THAT I AM, mighty I AM Presence
come forth
and surround me in the brilliant Tube of Light supreme.
May the Rays bring their service of light and sound.
May the Rays bring their service eternal in their protection of
I AM THAT I AM.

HIGHER REFINEMENT THROUGH THE VIOLET FLAME

When you call forth this Tube of Light, you are then prepared to call forth the Violet Flame. Use any decree that you feel you align with or feel a vibratory frequency towards. It is very important for you to see how, within that Tube of Light, the Violet Ray is not dissipated but it is held eternally with you throughout the day. This brings again, a greater vibrational upliftment and attunes your consciousness into a higher refinement. Of course, this is always what we are working towards, gathering light frequencies and sound frequencies, so they can be used for that greater service supreme. [See Appendix A, *The Three Standards.*]

Dear ones, Dear hearts, these are the three standards to start with. To bring an even greater alignment is to move into the Golden City Vortices. I have given much teaching on this and how they are also used to bring a higher frequency forward. However, for those chelas who cannot move into these sacred sites at this time, it is important to understand that a change within the diet and using the mighty Tube of Light, along with the Violet Ray, will bring forth a greater frequency in vibration.

THE CONNECTION WITHIN

As a chela is readied along the path, a time comes for a connection with a Master Teacher. As I have said so many times before, "when a student is readied, the Master appears." You know Dear chelas of mine, that moment when the Master Teacher came forward and said, "Can I now give you service?" For you see, that connection always happens, not through an external teacher or guru, but always happens from within.

EL MORYA'S MEDITATION TECHNIQUE

To gain that contact within, it is important to begin to learn meditation. One of the first and key moments to train the consciousness to respond to the quiet stillness is the simple candle reflection. Beloved El Morya has given this teaching several times but just to refresh your memories, I shall now give you continued discourse on this topic. [See Appendix B, *Candle Meditation*.]

When you light the candle and sit in front of it in quiet reflection and silence, you are seeing a light that shines within, are you not? When you notice the flame of that candle, you notice that there is a greater heat and light that comes from within. It is a great metaphor for understanding how the energy and the light bodies work upon the human.

The light bodies are a flame but within, is a greater heat or light that is generated. It is an unseen heat or force and of course, this is where we seek to gain our contact. This is the seating of I AM THAT I AM. It is that great Eight-sided Cell of Perfection that we have spoken of in many discourses. This Eight-sided Cell of Perfection contains within it the ability to enter into timelessness. In this moment, as we speak, as I give this teaching, have we not entered into a zone of eternal silence and timelessness? This of course is very important for the chela to understand. It is the supreme peace. It is the supreme At-ONE-Ment.

CONTACT WITH THE MASTER

In this unseen Sacred Fire exists the unity of all consciousness and it is in the understanding of this level of consciousness that the chela then begins to understand that all is connected in a mighty and grand Oneship. This eternal Source, this wellspring of creation, exists in all of life. But contact and understanding with the Source is most important to then gain contact with the Master Teacher. The Master Teacher prepares the consciousness a little at a time. Of course, the new chela cannot be immediately infused with these energies and vibrations, for it would be too much at that time for the chela to contain and hold within its light bodies.

Little by little, the Master Teacher comes at nighttime and guides the exit from the physical body into the dream space, to the great schools that reside in the Golden Cities. In these schools, the chela then is given greater instruction…instruction that entails past lifetimes…instruction in the source of all desires and all actions and is readied in a greater plan to bring contact with the Master Teacher into conscious awareness. This of course takes time indeed. Sometimes this process takes seven years total. But if the chela is accelerated through work that it has made in other lifetimes, sometimes this process happens within twenty-four hours and contact is achieved immediately. Now, the inner contact with that mighty teacher, the Master Teacher, is one that is sustained through lifetime after lifetime after lifetime. That is why the contact that we have Dear ones, Dear hearts, has been so strong and so powerful, for we have had an affiliation before, have we not?

Answer: *This is very true.*

MASTERY OF THOUGHTS, FEELINGS, AND ACTIONS

This contact has been very important, for it has brought forth a greater intention and a greater service. It is then through this greater service that the chela is brought one step at a time through a greater understanding of light and sound and brought into a greater service. However, before the chela can be used in a service for humanity, it must be brought into a greater understanding and Mastery of its own desires, of its own emotional body, and of its own thoughts. This is the Mastery of thought, feeling, and action. These simple principles are then brought into a greater integration and used for the chela. Sometimes this takes a very short time but sometimes, it takes a very long time.

SACRIFICE AS ENERGY FOR ENERGY

When the chela then is asked to perform some sacrifice, such as giving up meat or giving up any other material possession, this austerity allows the Master Teacher then to match energy for energy. When the Violet Flame is called upon, then the Master Teacher can come forward to give, matching their energy with the chela's energy. Even before we go into discourse, do you not call upon that Mighty Violet Flame? This Violet Flame brings forward a momentum of energy, as I have stated before. Thousands upon thousands recite that Mighty Violet Flame with you in one consciousness, in one voice, in one light and sound vibration.

There is that Law of Energy for Energy, so with each small sacrifice that the chela makes, the Master Teacher guides and leads that chela into a greater understanding, until, when the time is ready, there is a greater acceleration of vibration. There is a greater understanding and Unity Consciousness then achieved in its totality. Once this Unity Consciousness is achieved and one has entered into the grand palace beyond illusion, then the chela is ready to enter into the path of Ascension. Of course, I will not get into the details of the path of Ascension today but I wanted you to understand, Dear ones, Dear hearts, the procedures that lead the chela with the Master Teacher. Questions?

A DECREE TO BREAK ADDICTION

Question: *Is there a decree for the chelas so that they may dissolve and break the addiction to the animal products?*

Any Violet Flame Decree will work for this and that is why I have brought forward so many for you. But I shall give you one which will break down at a cellular level, the addicted desire for animal products:

Mighty Violet Flame blaze in through and around my being at the cellular level. Dissolve all connections to animal substances.
Dissolve all connections to addictive desires.
Mighty Violet Flame blaze, blaze, blaze eternal.
Mighty Violet Flame. Sacred Fire within me, burn, burn, burn forever.
Mighty Violet Flame come forth I AM.
Mighty Violet Flame forever I AM.

A SACRED WRITE AND BURN TECHNIQUE

Question: *Thank you. Is there also another decree for the individual who has a desire to have guidance from the Ascended Masters?*

It is best for this desire to be written down. It is best to refine the consciousness, as I have taught you in the write and burn techniques. [See Appendix C, *Write and Burn Method*.] This would be most appropriate for students who are desiring such inner instruction. It is important to write a letter and address it to the great I AM THAT I AM, stating such a desire within. Fold the letter and place it by the bed stand at night and it shall be delivered to the Violet Flame Angels and thereupon, taken to the Master Teacher. The great intention has been stated from the soul in the silence of "to do and to dare." Dear ones, Dear hearts, then in the morning, burn this great request; this allows a greater release for this request to come forward. Questions?

THE DOMINANT RAY OF THE ASTRAL BODY

Question: *Yes. In relocating to a Golden City, many have called and asked, "How do I know which one to go to?" Is there a decree that will help them in determining that true path or that true course for their spiritual evolution?*

Dear one, it is important to understand the vibration of the Ray Forces within. As it has well been noted, there is always a dominant Ray Force within the astral body, is there not?

Answer: *This is true.*

CALL FORTH THE RAY TO ACTION

This always shows the greater alignment of the service of the soul, its development in past lives, and where its natural tendencies shall be in this lifetime. This is an important process to understand, where that greater alignment to the Ray Forces is within the self. Of course, you have understood how to identify these Ray Forces, have you not, through astrology? But for those who wish not to do this, there are the decrees to call forth that mighty Ray Force into action:

> Beloved mighty I AM Presence,
> Come forth and blaze eternal the Rays of
> love, service, and action.
> Bring them forth from the heart of the Mighty Logos.
> Bring them forth in the name of I AM THAT I AM.
> May this Ray Force now come forward and
> serve the one law supreme,
> I AM THAT I AM.

Questions?

THE MASTER TEACHER ASSISTS THE CHELA

Question: *Thank you. As I understand it, when the student is ready to be of help or service, the Master Teacher can then also match, energy for energy, this help and service. Does not that service, being for the upliftment of all of humanity, then uplift the student as well?*

It is true Dear one, Dear heart, for the Master Teacher, no longer bound by time, no longer bound by the fruit of the physical body, is then able to work energy at another level, at another level beyond the comprehension and the understanding of the student. When the Master Teacher, no longer bound by the restraints of the physical, enters into the field of the chela, the Master Teacher then is able to lift, guide, and assist the chela into greater understanding and into greater awareness. Of course, much of this is achieved in the dream state and in the schooling that continues on an ongoing state. But there is also that which is brought into the conscious awareness. Sometimes this is through the corner of the eye. You will notice a flash of light. There will even be that Master who will put on a disguise of the Ray Forces and appear in an unassuming manner, asking a question of you in the physical, offering assistance in some peculiar, subtle, and unknowing way. This vibration comes forward to bring its service in a greater alignment to the Plan Divine.

The Master Teacher is readying the student to gather force unto himself or herself in the physical plane; for you see, your work is in the physical plane. You are given assistance through the other realms and other dimensions, spiritual energies in a way to give you understanding. These of course uplift you and develop the will. The will then is ready to gather unto itself the force, the readiness, and the Divine Willingness. Through this development of the will, the chela then achieves a greater understanding. Many of the ancient shamans who understood the Earth Forces also understood the great will, the choice, and the intention to work with the physical energies to raise the body beyond the limits of the flesh.

UNSEEN ENERGY

It is important then to understand that there are energies that are unseen. This is one of the first lessons that the chela receives as conscious activity. How are these energies intuited and understood? They are felt first through that great emotional body. But if the emotional body is clogged through the wounds of the past or through unfulfilled desires, it is then almost impossible to feel objectively. Instead, it is always experiencing, feeling, or intuiting subjectively through the filter of the past or through the desires and the wants of the future. Therefore, it is very important that these are cleared out through the work of the Violet Flame. This is why this is brought forward. Then the Master Teacher can come forward and give energy for energy to assist, so that the chela then is prepared to feel the more subtle energies. Questions?

COMPASSION HEALS THE EMOTIONAL BODY

Question: *Doesn't this perception start when one sees a greater picture than the self?*

It does indeed, Dear one. It starts through an understanding as simple as that candle meditation. It starts, as El Morya has said, in becoming one with the candle. In that Oneship is the development of compassion. This brings the emotional feeling of love to a higher understanding. Love is no longer fulfilling individual wants or needs but is expressing at the greater level of compassion. This then manifests a greater healing energy of the intuitive or feeling body. Questions?

SYMPATHETIC HARMONY AND THE LAW OF ATTRACTION

Question: *But all of this is driven by ones desire, is it not?*

It is true Dear one. Desire, in its higher understanding, is the uniting with the Source, for then you understand that all is connected as ONE. Individual desire brings a greater teaching when it is understood in its higher understanding. All is brought forward in its greater timing and intent. As stated before, "when the student is ready, the Master then appears." The Master that appears is of like vibration and well suited to that student. This comes through that principle of sympathetic resonance or sympathetic harmonies. You see Dear ones, you attract it to yourself. Questions?

Question: *So the student, who would have the great desire for love or compassion, would attract someone such as yourself, would they not?*

It is true that the student would bring unto itself that which it desired. Now for the students who harbor resentment, they would then attract teachers of experience, teachers that would bring forward an understanding for the release of resentments, for the release of the little hurts and wants. Of course, when one works with a Master Teacher, they are always instructed in the greater refinement. I have outlined these. The sacrifice and giving up through austerities in the diet, what does this affect? It affects your relationship with the Earth. Immediately, your whole relationship with Earth is changed, is it not, through that simple change in the diet?

Answer: *This is very true. You are less attached.*

SYNERGISTIC SUCCESS

You become not only less attached but a shift in consciousness is achieved. You begin to see things in a different way. It releases consciousness to a new point of perception. When one is asked to change something that is quite difficult at the time and then achieves that, there is a level of success, is there not?

Answer: *This is true.*

This brings a greater understanding, a greater vibration, and a greater harmony with the Master Teacher. Students are also instructed in the Tube of Light. They are instructed in meditation. They are instructed in the great Law of Unity. The Master Teacher comes forward with the teachings of the Violet Flame, which bring the release of the many wounds of the past. All these work simultaneously to bring a synergistic motion. It brings the student into a greater sympathetic harmony, a greater vibration. Students then notice that they no longer desire certain company or certain areas. They no longer have a vibration for certain habits and attitudes. Does this not then bring a whole new circle of influence within the chela?

Answer: *Very true.*

And this is how it is achieved, incrementally. Questions, Dear one?

THE ANIMAL KINGDOM

Response: *I have noted in myself that if I were to look into the eyes of a cow, a chicken, or a rabbit, that there is no way I could eat one. There is a sense that all things have a right to their evolution and their experience and they are not here just to serve my little wants or desires.*

The Animal Kingdom is another round of evolution. Of course, it is interrelated with the human but it also has its own scheme, its own vibration, and its own order. There are those animals that raise in consciousness and move into the realm of human evolution. There are those humans who then move on in their greater understanding and evolution, onward and onward. Now consciousness does not fall to the level of entering into the level of an animal again once it has achieved human consciousness. You have noted that many humans act like vicious animals and there are many wonderful and peaceful animals whose consciousness is much higher than the lowest of humans. This is brought again for an understanding of sympathetic harmonies and vibrations. Questions, Dear one?

Answer: *All of this really touches my heart.*

I bring forward my work from the heart of love. I bring forward my service through the I AM THAT I AM. Know Dear one, we are all connected as ONE.

Response: *Yes we are. We are all connected as ONE. At this point I have no further questions.*

Then Dear heart, I shall take my leave and come forward again at the appointed time for further discourse.

3

Stars of the Golden Cities
Saint Germain

Greetings beloveds, Dear hearts, on that mighty Violet Ray. I AM Saint Germain and as usual, I request permission to come forward.

Response: *Please Saint Germain, you are most welcome.*

MOMENTUM OF THE VIOLET RAY

There is much work to be done and as always, Dear ones, Dear hearts, I ask for you to tarry not with this work, for indeed it is of great import. There is much more education to be achieved among the masses and much for those students and chelas of mine. Dear ones, Dear hearts, of all the work to be achieved, the greatest is that alignment to the mighty Violet Ray. For you see, continual daily use of that mighty Violet Ray brings with it a great momentum and through this great momentum, transmutation and ultimate Alchemy of the soul is achieved. When you call upon that mighty Violet Ray in action, you call upon, not only this Law of Momentum, but you call upon other Ascended Beings, other angels of this mighty Violet Ray, and thousands of others who have gone before you, who bring this Ray into its mighty wondrous action.

Violet Ray come forth, Violet Ray I AM.
Violet Flame stream forth, mighty Violet Ray I AM.

Violet Ray stream forth into the hearts of man.
Violet Ray come forward,
I AM, I AM, I AM.

GOLDEN CITY GRID

Dear ones, Dear hearts, today's discourse will focus, not only upon continued information on the Golden Cities and their great Divine Intervention for humanity, but also we shall talk about several Earth Changes events and also upon that mighty grid of creation. You see Dear ones, Dear hearts, the Golden City grid was brought forward as a great Divine Intervention for humanity. It is through and among this grid that those Golden City Vortices are activated and bring forth their great service for humanity. We have given you teachings on each of the Doorways and now would like to give you teachings upon the Stars, or shall we say, the intention of each Golden City Vortex.

THE GOLDEN CITY STAR: EIGHT LEI-LINES

The Stars are the locations where eight lei-lines intersect in these Golden City Vortices. There, Dear ones, Dear hearts, is that great condensation of the Ray Force from the Great Central Sun, arcing itself to the core of your own solar sun and into the heart of the Earth. This mighty ray, streaming forth as the breath from the Mighty Logos, is then dispersed in that forward motion of the Vortex. Each of the Doorways brings forth their service and this Ray then is allowed to bring forward its own Ray in action and seat itself into the hearts of those who call it forward. You see Dear ones, Dear hearts. through the central portion and part of the Star of each of the mighty vortices, this Ray Force is then allowed to enter into the Golden Cities and begin its disbursement for the work at hand.

ALIGNMENT OF THE WILL

Each Ray Force brings forth a different annotation or a different connotation for the work that is to be achieved in the Golden Age. That mighty Blue Ray brings forward, not only a transformation in Gobean, but it also promotes a will in action to serve a greater Plan Divine. This mighty will, when one is aligned to it, brings forward that choice within to do, to dare, and to be silent. It is then and only then that communion with the great inner self is achieved and the will is aligned to a greater force and united to the Ascended Masters and the hierarchy for our work.

"AS ABOVE, SO BELOW"

The Ruby and Gold Ray brings forward in Malton, not only a greater fruition of service, it also brings forward a greater understanding of the soul and its Oneship, or Unana, with all of nature and the elemental state. Dear ones, Dear hearts, harmony with nature is always important, is it not? For then, all the laws that supersede that into the alignment of the spiritual worlds are then able to be understood. "As above, so below" is its greater understanding.

UNITE AS ONE HEART

That mighty Violet Ray brings forward, not only a united Brotherhood and Sisterhood in that Golden City of Wahanee, but it brings forward the ultimate path of compassion and understanding. This understanding is absolutely necessary in order to move one into the greater realms of collective consciousness; for then and only then, when one is able to understand their Brother or Sister, they will then unite as ONE heart. ONE heart is always the Law of the Violet Flame, is it not Dear ones?

"I AM AS ONE"

When you move into the Golden City of Shalahah, we see that great anchoring of the Green Ray. The Green Ray of course brings forth abundance and prosperity for all and healing at great transformational levels. The Green Ray also brings forward a wondrous thinking in scientific development. But this Green Ray brings healing which is true At-ONE-Ment. This At-ONE-Ment brings peace to the heart, does it not? This is the highest use of the Green Ray, "Om Sheahah. I AM as ONE," may peace reign supreme.

THE LAW OF COOPERATION

In Klehma, the work of the mighty White Ray is indeed a Ray of Cooperation, where we are all united in service and stand at the feet of the holiest of holies. Dear ones, Dear hearts, the White Ray brings forward its greatest service of purification, does it not? But as always, conflict that is resolved through the ultimate Law of Cooperation, is the work of this mighty White Ray and purification is then achieved. The soul is set ready to open the heart, not only of compassion, but to lead into the great purity of the fires of Ascension. This is the work of that mighty White Ray in action.

FIVE TEACHINGS OF SPIRITUAL ACCELERATION

As you see, I have given you five teachings. Each of these five teachings are achieved in each of the stars of the five Golden Cities of the United States. Each of these spiritual teachings have been brought forward as a great spiritual migration and when I say spiritual migration, there are those who will indeed physically locate to each of these Stars to seek that mighty Ray in action, to speak that mighty spiritual truth. But Dear ones, Dear hearts, migration itself is within, is it not? The teachings of the Inner Garden have always been given through Dear Sananda, to lead one into the inner self.

When one has contact with the great inner self, one then is ready to receive teaching at a greater level. It is important always to have this contact, for only through this contact can direct teachings with the Master Teacher then be achieved. This is indeed the first purpose of the Stars energies. Each of the Stars readies the student at a cellular and also a spiritual level into a greater acceleration and union with the Master Teacher who serves that Ray Force.

THE ASCENSION SPIRAL

Each of these Master Teachers comes forward in their thought, their intention, and their purity at this time, to lead the student and the chela into a greater understanding and a greater initiation. Each of these spiritual teachings becomes as an initiation, each leading higher and higher into that spiral of the chamber of the Ascension. It is there and only there that the student realizes that the flesh is limited. Only through working in the finer bodies is one then able to release the desires that trap one. This leads into a greater desire… that great desire of the Source…that great desire to know God…that great desire to become ONE with, at ONE.

APPEARANCE OF THE MASTERS

These Stars are also great locations for the Master Teacher and his entry into the Earth Plane and Planet. As it has always been prophesied, the Stars are indeed the locations where the Master Teachers shall and will appear in their physical, tangible bodies to give help and aid after the great purification. You see Dear ones, Dear hearts, there are many Earth Changes events that are destined to happen. As you well know, global warming has overtaken the entire Earth Planet and there have been those who know this indeed at your governmental circles. There have of course been those who have come forward trying to stop such an event but if you can see Dear ones, Dear hearts, everything has a purpose. As you well know, nothing happens by random choice. Everything, in its timing and intention, brings forward a greater understanding, a greater evolution.

GROWTH THROUGH THE EARTH CHANGES

As we have always said, it is through this great purification, through this great Earth Change, that humanity will be brought to a greater understanding of the self. And in this greater understanding of the self, is not the heart then opened? Is not then the opportunity for spiritual knowledge also opened as well? The great Earth Changes come forward as an opportunity for humanity to grow through this mighty law. It is only through this that one is challenged, that one then rises again to another level and is able to meet who they truly are. As I have always said, until one is ready to meet the true self, one is not ready to move beyond. One must be willing to face the true self, who they truly are, and only in understanding the true self is one then ready to face the Sacred Fire.

TRANSMUTING SELF-CREATED HELLS

We have spoken of this so many times, Dear ones, Dear hearts. The self begins its own self-created hell of judgment and condemnation of self. When you use this mighty Violet Ray in action, it brings forward the transmutations of the judgments of self and then one is ready to meet the true self, the mighty I AM Presence. This is the work of the Master Teachers in each of the Stars, to bring forward that meeting with the true self. At first this journey, this path to find the true self, is found through meetings in the astral planes… is found through meetings in meditation…is found through meetings in the dream state. But after the great Earth Changes, as each of these events unfold, as they have been given to you in the I AM America Prophecies, you will find that there will come a time beyond the Time of the Purification where the Master Teachers will come forward and serve in this greater initiation. Of course, it is important now, if you so choose, to begin this alignment process. Each one of these Ray Forces comes forward in their great intention from the Great Central Sun.

THE CONSENT OF BABAJERAN

This alignment process can be carried out, not only through the five Golden Cities of the United States, but can be continued on through all fifty-one of the great Golden Cities. This Golden City network is indeed a grid of consciousness that has been enacted through the complete cooperation of beloved Babajeran, Mother Earth, and the Ascended Masters. It was long decided, when it was known that these changes were coming, that a great Divine Intervention was in order if humanity was to move forward through such a change. There are of course those from other Star seeds, those from other galaxies, who have come at this time, hoping to interfere, hoping to upset the balance of karma upon this Earth Plane and Planet. But know this, Dear ones, Dear hearts, Dear stewards of this plan, this Divine Intervention will move forward because it moves forward with the consent of the Mother Planet.

THE GREAT PURIFICATION

This great purification moves forward for all the people of the Earth. It moves forward for all cultures and all races. It knows no boundary of religion…it knows no boundary of gender…it knows no boundary of economy or economic status…it knows no boundaries. That is why it comes forward in its great import. To bring this teaching of prophecy is to not hold back such a change but to fan that ultimate Flame of Freedom that resides in the human, soon to become the Divine God-man. [See Appendix D, *The Great Purification*.]

GIFT OF SPIRITUAL FREEDOM

Dear ones, Dear hearts, there are many who will make their Ascension in this great purification. As this great global grid is activated, so are many changes within the HU-man, the Divine God-man. There comes forward that great and mighty flame as it was always meant and intended to be. One then gains, as Dear Sananda has said, the great gift, the mighty gift of Ascension that awaits all of you. It awaits those in the Rapture…it awaits those in Revelation…it awaits those who understand light and sound…it awaits those as Jacob's ladder…it awaits many of those who are ready to move onward now into a greater plan…it awaits those who seek liberation…it awaits those who wish to cleanse the wheel of karma. As you see Dear ones, Dear hearts, it is indeed multicultural. It is a time that is intended for all of those who have the eyes to see and the ears to hear.

ACCELERATION IN THE STARS

Each of the Master Teachers will be serving in the Stars of these great and wondrous locations of Golden Cities. It is important also to note that prior to Earth Changes, a great acceleration is available for those who will travel to Stars and carry out their prayers, meditations, and intentions. That is why these locations have been given, so that those who are readied may come forward now to serve a greater Plan Divine. Those who are ready may now come forward and assist the Ascended Masters in this greater working.

When you enter into a Star, you will feel a higher frequency and a higher vibration. Of course, Dear ones, Dear hearts, this is the vibration of the Ray Force arcing itself from the central part of the white core of the Earth into the surface of the Earth. At first it enters through the bottom of the feet but then one hears and feels that great opening in the heart. In this opening of the heart to the Ray Force, one then begins to hear the high-pitched hum, a higher frequency, a higher vibration. For those who have a difficulty in hearing this vibration, it is important then to stay on a completely animal free diet for no less than five days before entering into the Star. You see Dear ones, Dear hearts, this higher frequency, this higher vibration, can then be much more easily felt. If you are having problems even then, call upon the mighty Violet Ray to bring forth its cleansing and transmutation. This higher frequency energy then comes forward to lead you onward to meet with the mighty I AM Presence.

AKASHIC HISTORY OF HUMANITY

As I have stated before, it is throughout all Golden Cities that the Akashic Records are present. You see Dear ones, Dear hearts, the Ascended Masters, in their great wisdom and knowing of this time of turmoil, filled each of the Golden Cities at a vibrational and energetic level with the Akashic Records of all of the history of humanity. For you see Dear ones, Dear hearts, there have been those who have tried to adulterate this history, so you would not understand the true divinity that lies within. When one is willing to search at a higher level, when one is ready to meet that deep resource from within, then and only then, does the wellspring of truth come forward. There are indeed the great schools that reside in the Golden City Vortices and those who have the eyes to see and the ears to hear can receive that greater knowledge.

THE GREAT MYSTERY SCHOOLS

Let me review these great schools of wisdom and knowledge for those who dare to do. In Gobean are the great mystery schools of Egypt. In Malton are the great mystery schools of Atlantis, that also contain the information related to the Celtic and the Druid cultures. In Wahanee are the great mystery schools of the ancient schools of Africa, that great culture that once existed over the entire Sahara

Desert. In Shalahah are the great mystery schools of the Vedas, those which align to ancient India. And in Klehma are the mystery schools that relate to the cultures of the Pleiades, those that are known as the Aztec and Incan cultures.

In Gobean, there is also a greater alignment during the opening of Shamballa. During this great time, this City of White opens its gates to bring forward a greater understanding of this mystery school. It is important to understand how the five schools will serve those in the United States and also serve those who travel to them to seek this knowledge. At a later date, I shall open more information regarding the other mystery schools to be opened but for now this information is indeed enough, Dear ones, to absorb.

GOLDEN CITY NETWORK

The Golden City grid is one of many grids that exist over the Earth Plane and Planet. As we have stated before, the Golden City grid is created through the complete cooperation and harmony of beloved Mother Earth and the Ascended Masters. There is also that mighty Map of Rings and this indeed vibrates from the fourth layer of the field of the Earth. The Golden City grid vibrates from the fifth layer of the field of the Earth. It is important to understand this, Dear ones, Dear hearts, for there is other information that is being given to other channels now, to other students of the hierarchy, on other grids that exist. Know this Dear ones, Dear hearts, that not one grid is in conflict with the other but yet they all work together to serve a greater Plan Divine. They all work together to serve a greater harmony that comes forward during this time of massive change.

You see Dear ones, Dear hearts, there will be many volcanic eruptions that are soon to happen upon the Earth Plane and Planet. These of course bring forward a greater activation of many of the grids and we shall see more subsequent activations of the Golden City network and grid. It is important Dear ones, Dear hearts, to understand each and every one of the lei-lines, those that not only intersect to create that mighty Star in action, but also those that intersect to create each of the gateways. For you see Dear ones, these also serve minor or sub-vortices that exist on the vortex itself. I shall give more information about these in later teachings. It is important now for you to study these locations and to see how they will serve a greater Plan Divine. And now, I shall open the floor for your questions.

RAY FORCES AND STAR SEEDS

Question: *Since each of the Golden Cities contains the resonance of a specific ray, are there different groups of people that will be attracted to each of these Ray Forces?*

It is true Dear ones, Dear hearts, that in the individual embodiment, there is one Ray Force that comes forward to bring a greater teaching, a higher learning to that individual. However, there is always the Golden City that the soul itself is attracted to. Of course, this comes forward from the premise and idea of the Star seed. The Star seed shows, not only a genetic lineage, but also shows a lineage of spiritual teachers or, shall we say, of the sponsor teacher. One is drawn to be with their sponsor teacher. One is also drawn to be with their Master Teacher. The Master Teacher is the teacher who has been chosen to guide and lead that chela or student in that embodiment. The sponsor Master Teacher is the guardian of that being throughout many, many embodiments and is there to lead one into the path of Ascension, into the greater Service Divine. A Master Teacher may work, not only through one embodiment, but several and also use the assistance of different spiritual guides and other spiritual teachers who may come forward. Questions?

LEVELS OF HARMONY

Response and question: For many individuals wanting to know where to relocate, it has always been my advice that they go inside and find a place that they have a sense of love for and that will be their answer for relocating. Is there more that you can add to this?

All follows that greater Law of Harmony Divine. Have you not noted Dear one, that when things fall into place quickly, easily, readily, that this is the first key, is it not? It is the clue that all has come forward in a greater alignment, into a greater harmony. First always, observe the level of harmony, for then and only then, may the Laws of Abundance and true Prosperity bring forth their manifestation. But know this Dear ones, Dear hearts, that all is brought forward always on the premise of the greater sacrifice. There are always those who wish, who desire, but yet are never willing to match energy for energy. Know this too is true.

SPIRITUAL INITIATION AND COLLECTIVE CONSCIOUSNESS IN THE GOLDEN CITY

Question: Are there signs, specific Earth Changes, we should look for, to know that it is time for all of us to move to these areas?

It is important first Dear ones, Dear hearts, to move into the teachings of the heart. First, realize that you are indeed all as ONE. You all are interconnected as one great consciousness. This teaching is most important, for when you enter into the Golden City, this will bring a greater understanding to that first level of initiation. There are many changes that will happen in the next ten to twelve years upon the Earth Plane and Planet. Know that the global warming will accelerate and bring greater super storms to the Earth Plane and Planet. These super storms will not be denied and you will see them reported within your media, some of them very shocking indeed.

But let us not put our focus upon physical manifestations for now. Let us put our focus upon the spiritual manifestation. Let us put our focus upon the longing of the heart and the urgings within.

Not only should one focus upon that mighty Law of ONE, one should also focus upon the Law of Transmutation, Mercy, and Forgiveness, as I have stated before, that mighty Violet Ray. For then and only then can that mighty Green Ray of healing come forward and bring a greater harmony of self…a greater prosperity to the being…a greater harmony within life. Then and only then is one prepared properly to move into the collective consciousness that is contained within Unana and that mighty White Ray. Yes indeed, there are the disharmonies that must be faced, the trials and tribulations to be overcome. But as I have said before Dear ones, Dear hearts, it was never promised to be easy. More questions?

WHERE WE GO ONE, WE GO ALL

Question: *Yes. Within this Oneness, we are ONE with you and other members of the hierarchy, is this not so?*

It is so Dear ones, Dear hearts. As one moves forward, even just one within one group, is not the whole group also moving forward? This is the statement of the unity and collective consciousness of Unana: As one moves forward, the whole group also receives the benefit. This is the work of Mass Ascension, global ascent, and the Rapture. As one moves forward, two then shall join, then more and more and more.

THE ASCENSION VALLEYS

Question: *Are we to achieve this specifically in Golden Cities or in the Ascension Valley locations?*

The Ascension Valley location was given so that one could begin to understand a greater condensation of this energy. For you see Dear ones, Dear hearts, when one would enter into such an energy field, one would be accelerated almost at a compatible level to that of traveling to the Star of Klehma. As I stated before, there are many other locations across the globe.

Question: *Is this the appropriate time to give any of those or is that in the future?*

That shall be released in its own timing and intent. But for now, this one location is given for those who wish to go to achieve this greater acceleration. However, know this, that those who wish to travel to the Star of Klehma would also note a similar energy, for indeed these two energy centers are aligned.

STARS AND INTERCONNECTIVITY

Question: *I see. So, it is your recommendation that those who have the desire, those who have the longing, should travel to the Stars of the Vortices. Is this not so?*

It is so Dear one, Dear heart. Of course, it is more difficult to live within a Star, for you see, these Stars are all interconnected with one another. One may begin to feel the great purification in the movement of Mother Earth and begin to know the Mother Earth as a great Cosmic Being. This interconnection in the Stars of all Golden Cities produces that greater movement into Unity Consciousness. But as you well know, one must be properly prepared before they enter into such an initiation.

INTEGRATION AND THE FOUR DOORWAYS

Response and question: *Yes, I do know this well. So those who visit these Golden Cities will find an expansion and a new inner connectedness to the planet and the hierarchy. Is this not so?*

It is true Dear ones. This is where the Akashic Records can be opened, for those who wish to receive that inner instruction. But for those who wish to move to Golden Cities, Eastern Doorways are always the best; for there, the energies are more pure and readily assimilated. From there, you can migrate to the Southern Door. Those who wish to have businesses, to carry on commerce, can migrate then to the Northern Door. The Western Door, as we have always stated, is for that higher intention to integrate the energies received from the great Akashic Records from the schools that reside "as above, so below." But those who wish to integrate the energies and to move into ceremonial order can travel and spend a few days within the Star.

Question: *As each of the Stars has a quality and a Ray Force and each of the Doorways has its own quality, is it advisable for those who wish to assimilate that quality or to transmute a portion of that quality in themselves, to use that criteria to determine which location to visit?*

It is always from within Dear one, Dear heart. As I have stated before, each one feels their particular alignment to a Master Teacher. Each one feels a particular alignment to the culture, to the school that resides above. Each one feels a longing within. There are even those who are placed there, as they thought, through serendipity but indeed there is no random act, is there ever, Dear one, Dear heart? For those who have not received instruction at the inner level of where they shall go, call upon me and there I AM. I shall always lead one into that greater alignment, as their Dear Brother and friend.

VIOLET FLAME DECREE FOR THE GOLDEN CITY JOURNEY

Question: *Is there a specific invocation for your assistance in this journey?*

>Mighty Violet Ray come forth in the name of
>I AM THAT I AM.
>Bring forth the alignment of my will to the Divine Plan.
>Show forth the work of the Violet Flame
>what I am to bring forward.
>Show forth the work of this Violet Ray,
>the mighty greater plan.

Response and question: *Thank you. That will be most helpful. So those who would be drawn to the Akashic Records of Egypt and would have a desire in their heart to meet Master El Morya would be going to Gobean, and so forth with the Records of Atlantis and Kuthumi in Malton, and the great African cultures and yourself in Wahanee. Is this not so?*

As I have stated before, Dear ones, each of the Master Teachers stands forward to bring their service. Of course, they are always assisted by the beloved Archangels and the beloved Elohim, but call upon me and there I AM. Questions?

Response: *I have no further questions at this moment regarding the discourse that you have brought forward. And I would like to close at this moment for this part of the discourse.*

So Be It, Dear ones.

4

Ascension of Consciousness
Saint Germain

Greetings Beloved chelas in that mighty Violet Ray. I AM Saint Germain and I stream forth on that Violet Ray of Mercy, Compassion, and Forgiveness. As usual Dear hearts, I request permission to come forward.

Response: *You have our permission Saint Germain, please come forward.*

CAUSE AND EFFECT

There is much work for us to continue with Dear ones, Dear hearts, within this dispensation, not only of that Mighty Violet Ray but also of that Mighty Green Ray. The work that you are bringing forward, while it contains many aspects of that mighty Violet Ray of Transmutation, Alchemy, ultimate Compassion, and Forgiveness, it also contains within it that Green Ray of Understanding. For you see Dear ones, Dear hearts, it was long decided that there would be brought forth a dispensation to bring an understanding of cause and effect to humanity. This has now been brought forth in the teachings of prophecy but also in the teachings of the energetic grids, the layers of the field of the aura and the layers of the field of the Earth. When all of this is brought to a greater understanding, then healing can come forward. This healing that comes forth from the heart of the Central Sun, that mighty logos, aligns to the Divine Plan, to that mighty will. OM MANAYA, PITAYA, HITAKA!

ALIGNMENT AND HARMONY

Dear ones, Dear hearts, this healing work that comes forward brings a greater alignment of that mighty will among the collective consciousness of humanity. It is this alignment of the will that is of most importance and you know that this has been the focus and the intention of the work in Gobean and the work of beloved Master El Morya. This mighty Blue Ray, as it streams forth from the heart of the Central Sun, arcing through the solar system to the core of your own Earth, brings with it an understanding and an intention to bring others to that greater plan . . . to a greater alignment . . . to their own purpose in this embodiment.

When one enters into this path of greater purpose and alignment to that Divine Plan, a greater harmony then ensues. This harmony brings forth an easing in the collective consciousness. The tensions begin to ease and balance begins to come forth from the great heart of compassion. This balance, when it is understood, brings a greater opening of the heart of love and a greater peace and tolerance is the end result. This grand alignment brings a greater energy over the Earth. This energy, when it is understood as a greater cosmic unity, begins to align with greater ease to the solar system. That alignment to the solar system brings forth a greater alignment to the Great Central Sun.

"LOVE, IN ACTION"

As you see Dear ones, these three actual physical locations are always working to bring a greater harmony for the evolution of those on planet Earth. This alignment also brings a greater understanding of the positioning of the Earth as a schoolroom. As it has always been said, "To do, to dare, and to be silent." Those who enter into the Earth Plane understand the great need to bring demonstration into the physical . . . understand the great need to bring forth action . . . understand the great need to put love into complete and total action. As we have always stated before, it is love in action, is it not, that brings about that greater understanding, that greater education?

When one begins to understand the intention of their heart and brings this intention further into its greater plan and awareness, the schoolroom becomes, shall we say, a great flora and fauna of experience. To love brings about a completion, does it not? To love brings about a greater understanding of the emotional fields and a greater understanding of higher intelligence and how this higher intelligence can be brought into greater thinking and arenas of experience. Through this greater plan, the Law of Love, all is brought to greater alignment and to greater harmony and ultimately, a greater abundance. This grand alignment upon the Earth Plane and Planet brings about a graduation of souls upon this schoolroom. This graduation of course is not just a graduation in consciousness but also a graduation that leads one to a greater understanding of the Ascension.

HEALING AND THE ASCENSION

The Ascension, as you see Dear ones, Dear hearts, is the movement, yes, interdimensionally but it is also a greater and higher awareness of experience. The Ascension of consciousness brings a greater understanding of the purpose of the Law of Love and the inter-connectivity of all in your path. Compassion, which is an element and an aspect of that mighty Violet Ray, brings forward a greater understanding of the Law of Love. One then is readied and able to see that great inner working in all situations and circumstances. As I have said before, there is never a mistake, ever, ever, ever. When one enters into that mighty Law of Compassion, one is then able to see how this mighty law works in the Earth Plane and Planet and brings one into a higher awareness, into a higher experience of consciousness. This of course is the path of Ascension and many who work on that mighty White Ray understand and know that the healing of many wounds is always essential in order to bring one to a higher consciousness. But this healing, does it not come forward through the letting go of past experience?

SPIRITUAL EDUCATION

This letting go is not forgetting the lesson but forgetting the pain and moving beyond the experience that is encoded in the memory. The memory is then viewed with the end result, as I have always said, of education. This grander education exists for all upon the Earth Plane and Planet. It is the purpose of life here . . . it is the purpose that one is moving towards . . . moving to a greater education . . . having a greater knowledge of the inter-connectivity that exists within that mighty Law of Love. When you call upon that mighty Violet Flame, it leads you into a greater awareness, a greater tolerance of experience, and expands one in that mighty heart of love into the consciousness of Unana, into the consciousness of that all and mighty ONE.

KARMIC PATTERNS

In the consciousness of the all and mighty ONE, lies the memory eternal, lies the true memory that exists in all situations and circumstances. This is important to understand as one enters into that focused path of Ascension, that all experiences are inter-connected, each to the next. Yet, all experiences are seen for the unity that they contain, seen through that one thread or path of demonstration that they hold. This path of course is the path of love, for one then sees the tolerance, the open giving. The open door, as Dear Sananda has always expressed, is contained in all experiences. When the soul is non-detached from these experiences, it is very hard to let go of the wounds of the past and the soul is held back in its own evolution. The soul is then called upon to repeat the experience over and over again. While some might see this as a punishing effect of karma, know Dear ones, Dear hearts, it is no punishing affect at all but only the exercise of your will and your choice. These repeat performances, shall we say, of experiences are seen at a point in evolution as a pattern.

"THE REWARD IS IMMEASURABLE"

These patterns of course are very important for the development of the will and the soul. Through this experience and demonstration of end results, one is then able to align through choice to a higher experience. This higher alignment and the use of that mighty Blue Ray brings transformation. This transformation is always essential Dear ones, Dear hearts, in order to move to a greater understanding of a pattern. These patterns of past experience are held by all who tread the spiritual path. All will begin to understand through that end result, education. Being led through the experience of a painful existence, education always comes to the forefront, does it not? For we have always stated, it is never promised to be easy but the reward is immeasurable. That is why those who tread the path to higher knowledge . . . who seek Ascension of their own consciousness . . . who seek an Ascension of any situation or circumstance are then led into the embrace of the mighty Violet Ray.

REVIEW YOUR PATTERNS

When one reviews, through meditation or in calmness of their day, the past karmas, or actions of that day, one then can see the result of patterns, many patterns of the past that are held at many levels. These patterns are held in the physical body, yes, but they are also held in that most important body of understanding, the mental body. For in that mental body is contained, at all times, the mighty builder of the physical form. It is true Dear ones, when you put your focus there, you shall see the end result. I have taught this many, many times in my precipitation and manifestation techniques.

It is important to understand that thoughts do create physical end results. Of course, this being a primary entry lesson for those upon the path of the Ascension, it is always important to give this great review, to understand that there is always an end result to an action. The action, does it not always come from the mental functions? Does it not come forth through thinking such a thing first? Thoughts must be held to be more sacred, Dear ones, Dear hearts. Thoughts that are held then seek a manifestation through that natural law. All thoughts will contain an end result. Of course, then one says, "How do I capture the mind? How do I keep the mind from traveling and racing into undesired areas? How do I harness the energy of my mind? How do I bring my mind forward into a greater alignment to the Divine Will?"

THE HEART AND SACRED FIRE

The mind itself is always balanced through that mighty heart of love and in that heart of love is the consciousness of the ONE, Unana. The mind is brought to a quietness, is it not, through the use of that Sacred Fire, the mighty Violet Ray? This is why we have brought these techniques forward at this time, Dear ones, Dear heart, so the mind can be tamed as it travels through the experience of illusion. Illusion is indeed a topic to be understood, is it not? For then one sees the temporal illusion of the creation of the mind and the temporal illusion of the experiences of the physical.

BEYOND ILLUSION

Illusion exists, Dear one, to bring the education of the truth . . . to bring you into the alignment of the mighty Law of Love . . . to bring you into the alignment of that Plan Divine. One then begins to peer above illusion, when having the experience of Divine Love. One then begins to have experiences beyond illusion, when seeing the cause of unity demonstrating in all experience. These indeed are the true treasures that await the one who ascends upon the spiritual path . . . who ascends in consciousness . . . who ascends in understanding . . . who ascends to that mighty alignment—the love of all—that guides humanity.

INVOKE THE FLAME

This mighty Violet Ray streams forth too as the Blue Ray comes forward. This mighty Violet Ray streams forth from the heart of the Great Central Sun, arcing itself to the solar sun, then to core of the Earth. As you invoke its substance, it comes forth from the ethers. As it appears, coming from each layer of the field of the Earth, it is contained within its own manifestation. When you command and demand a Ray Force into action, you are calling, not only upon that Law of Love, but also upon a law that exists within the physical. For you see, all the Rays in their action come forth at every level, as well as the same level of your experience of mind into physical manifestation.

TAMING EMOTIONS

Then one is led to ask, "What about the emotional field? Is not all thought, then feeling and action?" Of course, Dear ones, it is but the feeling is brought more to bridge the thought and the action. It is always that great impetus that then brings the will to action, does it not? The emotions have always been so important to understand and the taming of the emotions is as important as the taming of the mind. For the mind, when we see with crystal clarity, we can see each individualized thought as it passes through the mind. But it is the nature of the human to get trapped upon occasion in the fields of emotional experience. Why is this so?

Held within the genetic coding is the genetics of the animal in the experience upon the Earth Plane and Planet. This is not to say that the human is animalistic but, at times, can behave and act in an animal behavior or modality. It is always a matter of choice, is it not Dear ones, Dear hearts? Calling upon that Will Divine, raises one to a higher understanding, to a greater knowledge. Then in that greater knowledge, one begins to understand that the travails among the illusions are indeed controlled through the mental out-picturing.

GROWTH THROUGH EXPERIENCE

All experiences come, of course, through the mental conduit of out-picturing. This is the basis Dear ones, Dear hearts, of manifestation and experience. Through this out-picturing, the soul in its sojourn in the Earth Plane and Planet grows, learns, and receives the most precious gem of all—education. Where does this all fit in, one may ask, lifetime after lifetime? The soul, ascending upon the spiritual path, learns that education is the highest reward.

Dear ones, Dear hearts, as you understand, the Earth schoolroom is a place where you grow only by experience, only by demonstration in the physical. The astute student begins to understand, through these experiences, that there is a higher order which brings about the patterns, demonstrating great physical laws. There is indeed a higher intelligence, is there not? There is indeed a higher order, is there not?

When one begins to see this higher order, they begin to understand the Ascension of consciousness and there is much more that lies beyond physical demonstration and the Maya or illusion. There is the eternal truth that lies behind all such things, even behind that of the mind . . . a Divine Order that is being orchestrated beyond a great central intelligence. Dear ones, Dear hearts, when one begins to seek this great higher order, they are then ready to meet the I AM THAT I AM.

THE MIGHTY I AM PRESENCE

The first of the I AM THAT I AM is the God-self that dwells within. It has always been there but it lies, shall we say, asleep within so many people. It is not yet awakened, not yet put in its proper authority. When one begins their contact with this mighty I AM, one then begins to see the spiritual laws that lie underneath all activity . . . the true realities that lie within all situations and circumstances. When you travel in the physical experience in contact with the mighty I AM Presence, one then is led beyond illusion and into truth eternal. The contact with the mighty I AM indeed is the Akashic Record . . . indeed is the silent witness . . . indeed is that wellspring of eternal truth. The mighty I AM, Dear ones, Dear hearts, strives in the Ascension of consciousness to gain emotional and ultimate contact. The mighty I AM is contained within all. It contains within it, not only the universal mind but the universal heart of love. It contains within it all experiences, so it can lead you into new experience. Questions?

THE AWAKENING POINT

Question: *Yes. It is my impression that Ascension can only be taught to a mortal person by an already Ascended Being. Is this true?*

It is very difficult for the consciousness to be brought into its ascending order without the guidance of one who has been there before. However, within healing is the ultimate authority. That ultimate authority longs to be awakened . . . longs to be brought to the complete, full podium of consciousness. This awakening is always fostered by one who has been there before. As we have always said: To do, to dare . . . and then that great silence is the mighty witness.

Response: *I see. Then truly, Ascension occurs when the individual soul is sponsored by one who has already ascended.*

It is true Dear ones, Dear hearts. As you have understood before, there is always the sponsor who comes forward to begin that awakening process within the human. First, the animal behaviors are taken to the forefront, so that one may then be able to see the action of such. It is only through seeing ones animalistic instincts and behaviors that one is then able to call upon the mighty Divine Nature of choice and the engendering of the will. It is important Dear ones, Dear hearts, that when the sponsor comes forward, it is brought, shall we say, in the silence of a whisper. That awakening point, the birth of conscience, is most important.

BEYOND THE PHYSICAL

Response: *Yes, I understand. So, as I present some of the principles that you have shared with me with others, it will still require someone such as yourself to sponsor them in the Ascension.*

It brings one to a higher understanding of Unity Consciousness. For you see Dear ones, Dear hearts, in the awakening process, one is always at odds with the ego. Of course, the ego works for the greater purpose of presenting the mirror, or shall we say, the duad, to the soul in its educational process. It is important of course to be able to see how all is inner connected to the ONE. When one is not bound through the physical and not bound through time and space, there is an opportunity for a greater intervention. This greater intervention comes forward in its own timing and intention. There is not one, bound in the physical, who could completely understand this in its entirety.

To work beyond physical constraint and beyond time and space, you begin to understand, through the help of your sponsor, your Master Teacher, that relationship of the guru to the chela. Has it not been brought to you Dear ones, Dear hearts, that you can see what exists beyond time and space and what exists beyond the physical? You see these demonstrations brought forth daily and while each is brought with a physical result, you can also understand its intention and purpose behind and beyond the physical. It is important to understand that when one is not bound by these constraints, there is a fresh perspective. One is then allowed, as you so well know, to "hang on to that elephant" in a whole different manner.

THE ASCENSION PROCESS

Question: *Then as I understand it, the Ascension process is ongoing; it is not just from this realm but from the realm that you are residing in, by your sponsors?*

It is indeed, Dear ones, Dear hearts, for consciousness is ever expanding and growing. It moves beyond, even from its point of birth. And while this principle is taught in the physical, it is not a principle from the physical. The physical was given, Dear ones, as a great gift, so you could see each spiritual principle and how it is applied.

ASCENSION AND DIET

Response: *I understand. With regard to the mental body, emotional body, and action body, it's my impression and observation that the emotional body seems to be infinitely more active and overpowering than the mental body or the action body.*

As I have said before, the time period that the Earth is in, which is a time of lesser light, the emotions run quite rampant. These emotions are held in animalistic behavior and animalistic activity. That is why we have asked for the chelas, who wish to bring their consciousness to a momentum of Ascension, to limit their intake of animal products. The day-by-day ordered routine of Ascension necessitates the control of animalistic behavior and the animalistic genetic coding, a coding that has occurred through the intervention of other Star seeds upon the Earth Plane and Planet. You see Dear ones, Dear hearts, this control can be brought about through the simple principle of energy flows where attention goes. Now, how would this relate to the food that you eat? It is very simple when one understands a spiritual principle brought into physical order, is it not?

Response: *This is true. If you are partaking of animal products, then you are going to increase the energy of that within your own system.*

As I have explained before Dear ones, Dear hearts, to bring the consciousness to a higher order, to a higher understanding, we have brought this law eternal. Of course there are those who feel a great restriction in this. However, as I have always assured you, often through restriction, one then begins to become fully free. This freedom is one that is not understood until one has had the experience. I have always said Dear ones, Dear hearts, take this into the great laboratory of the self. Bring it into at least a six-week experiment and see for yourself if your consciousness does not have a higher and a finer quality. Is this not true?

DIVINE LOVE

Response and question: *I can attest to this being true in my own life. I have a question in regard to Divine Love. It has been my impression that, though ever present, Divine Love needs to be accepted to be activated in the consciousness. It seems that so many people deny this acceptance or seem to be attached to the concept of being unworthy. Could you comment on this?*

Divine Love always brings forth a greater enlightenment, does it not? For through the experiment and experience of Divine Love, one then is brought to a higher level of acceptance and a higher level of tolerance. This allows the thoughts then to become freed. Thoughts are freed beyond restriction . . . thoughts are freed beyond doubt . . . thoughts are freed beyond superstition . . . thoughts are freed beyond fear. Divine Love brings forward, in its emotional quality, a freeing of the mental body. Creations then can come forward from a higher order and a higher understanding. When one accepts this higher Law of Divine Love, one then begins to expand in their mental characteristics and expand in their day-to-day thoughts and thinking. These day-to-day thoughts then begin to create new experiences, do they not? These new experiences then begin to reflect and mirror back a greater order, a greater understanding beyond the ego, beyond illusion.

It is through Divine Love and the acceptance of Divine Love that all are loved, accepted, and needed . . . that all have their right to be here . . . that all have their right to have this experience . . . that all have their right to come forward in their own evolution. Divine Love sustains, maintains, protects, nurtures, and ultimately qualifies all to a higher order. Only through Divine Love does all then exist, does it not Dear one?

ACTION AND THE VIOLET FLAME

Response and question: *Yes, without a doubt. I have come to accept that the Divine Plan, Divine Will, and Divine Love are always in action. Another question, if one wishes to go forward and create something new, we have talked about the out-picturing process, but if one wants to be released from something, the only process that I am aware of is the utilization of the Violet Flame. Does this work completely with paying a debt or eliminating karmic attachments that you may find unpleasant?*

There are those who are more attached to their experience of pain than to the education contained therein. It is important of course to always call forth that mighty Violet Ray into any situation and circumstance where you wish to be freed. However, there are also many lessons that come forward, do they not, through the physical? Many lessons are able to be shown to you clearly and succinctly. Money or, shall we say, the attachment to money, is one of these. The attachment at the mental level and through the emotional experiences of feeling secure or insecure, are one way that one becomes over attached. Money is given, shall we say, to clarify the emotional body, so that one may become more clear in their intention with the physical.

EMOTIONAL ATTACHMENTS

It is important, when you are working to become free from such emotional attachments, to not only call upon the Violet Ray, but to use all write and burn techniques. The write and burn techniques not only call upon a level of transmutation and Alchemy but they require a physical action to begin to overcome the circumstances and situations brought about through emotional imbalance. When one becomes, shall we say, stuck within this muck and mire of emotion, it is important then to take action at a physical level. This physical activity is focused and directed always through the intention of the mind. Calling forward the higher order of the mind to identify the emotional response can bring a greater level of physical activity. Do you understand?

Question: *It is a form of out-picturing that will then take the life into an action, is what you are saying?*

It is true Dear one. Work first with the Violet Ray to identify the emotional responses, then use the write and burn techniques to eliminate these emotional responses that are overplaying in patterns. Man and money becomes stuck in emotional securities . . . stuck in power plays . . . stuck in happiness or unhappiness, contingent upon the amount of security contained in the physical world. Now, for the one who is traveling along the path of ascending consciousness, can you clearly see how this would indeed impede and hold one back?

Response: *It most certainly would.*

Do this work, Dear chela of mine, and I shall bring forth further assistance.

Response: *Yes.*

ENERGY FOR ENERGY

As you have understood Dear one, all comes forward from the Master Teacher energy for energy. It is true indeed through Divine Love that the sponsor comes forward and fans that flame, awakening the I AM to a greater level of understanding. But it is the Master Teacher who comes forward then and helps through this mighty Principle Divine.

EMOTIONS AND THE VIOLET FLAME

Question: *I see. Isn't it the emotional body that brings up memories and keeps us from being lulled into a state of unawareness and non-sensitivity?*

The emotional body plays its role in allowing the patterns to come forward, that then indeed spark the will to greater action and activity. But the emotional body itself can become out of balance with experiences that are judged as negative or positive. As I have stated before, it is important to use the Violet Flame to allow this sense of judgment of good versus bad, good versus evil, or negative versus positive, a greater understanding. That experience is there for the engendering of the will and moving the soul further on the path into the Ascension of consciousness.

Response: *That would make the most sense. At this point, I have no further questions.*

I should also like to remind you Dear ones, Dear hearts, that I will bring forward more information upon the Green Ray. For you see, today I have laid a template down which shall explain to you the beginning of the Blue Ray and the ultimate Alchemy of the Violet Ray. We have also introduced the premise of the mind, which is enlightenment brought from the premise of Divine Love. Now, we have the building blocks for that Mighty Green Ray of healing, do we not Dear ones, Dear hearts? In our next discourse, I shall bring further explanation. In that mighty Christ, SO BE IT!

Response: *So Be It!*

5

Temples of Consciousness
Saint Germain

Greetings beloveds in that mighty Violet Ray. I AM Saint Germain and I stream forth on that mighty Violet Flame of Mercy, Transmutation, and Forgiveness. As usual Dear hearts, I request permission to come forward.

Response: *Please, you are most welcome, come forward*

THE PATH OF FORGIVENESS

It is in that mighty Violet Ray that I stream forth in this work. It is through that Violet Ray, through Mercy, Compassion, and Forgiveness, that I am allowed to bring this information to you. It is only through that path of forgiveness that one then sees the higher reality, the higher explanation, the higher understanding in all things. Dear ones, Dear hearts, when you bring this application into your world, it is a Divine Law in action. In, through, and around this Divine Law is that mighty Violet Flame blazing its eternal path of forgiveness…blazing forever within you…blazing ever eternal. Dear ones, Dear hearts, this Violet Flame brings forth, not only a great Alchemy of the soul, it also brings forward a greater transmutation of the being. It is then able to bring that Divine Intervention into all actions of the past and bring them into an understanding, or a detachment, so you may then move into the present. This indeed does affect your future, does it not Dear ones? For as you well know, it is thought, feeling, and action, all combined together, that then creates the world in which you live.

It is important too to understand Dear chelas, students of mine, and to share with others, that in the work of prophecy there is always that element of choice. All that I have given to you about the future are indeed not predictions, but prophecies. When you begin to understand prophecy in its fullest context, you will then understand that it is through the collective consciousness that all is created. This great Co-creation is changing all the time, is it not, Dear ones, Dear hearts? Each individual thought, feeling, and action creates a momentum unto itself and that great collective consciousness then is formed.

COLLECTIVE CONSCIOUSNESS AND CHANGE

I have explained to you how this collective consciousness plays a role in creating these types of events that are prophesied to happen. However, prophecy is always given in that nick-of-time, so that things can be changed for a greater outcome…things can be changed for a greater intention…things can be changed to match a greater Co-creation. That is why the work of beloved Babajeran, along with that with Spiritual Hierarchy, is of the greatest importance. It is great to understand in this moment of time, the work of the Golden City Vortices, their great function, and how they bring about that Divine Intervention.

SPIRITUAL FUNCTION OF THE GOLDEN CITIES

Many times I have given you lessons and discourses about the Golden Cities, describing to you their function…giving you the proper instruction for each of the lei-lines and each of the gateways…how the Stars function, how they move, and how they interact with the core of the Earth itself…how this interaction extends out into the universe, arcing its energy to your solar force and onward to the Great Central Sun. But Dear ones, Dear hearts, it is also important to understand their spiritual function. This has been a very important aspect of this lesson. So now Dear ones, Dear hearts, I would like to share this information with you.

The Golden Cities were originally brought forward to preserve areas upon the Earth that could still receive, at a Fourth and a Fifth Dimensional level, higher spiritual energies. These higher spiritual energies are the energies that are used by the Ascended Masters, the Spiritual Hierarchy, and this Lodge of the Great White Dove. It is also so important to understand that this protection was brought forward also in cooperation with Mother Earth, beloved Babajeran. This instruction comes forward so that one can understand that if humanity chooses, through the collective consciousness, to enter into the Time of the Great Purification, the Time of the Great Earth Changes, that these areas would then be preserved to leave an imprint of higher energy for those to follow at a later date. However, as we all know, thought, feeling, and action create this greater template of creation. We shall see now what way humanity plans in its great choosing, what way it continues and moves forward in this grander Co-creation.

Dear ones, Dear hearts, these locations were also given to ensure a greater harmony and a greater instruction for those who have the eyes to see and the ears to hear...those who have the calling from within...those who, shall we say, thirst for that drink within. Each of the Golden Cities thus are sponsored by an Ascended Master Being, Elohim, or an Archangel, alongside their Ray Force, which is its complementary energy, as you know, from the Great Central Sun. These areas are very large indeed and become their own Temples of Initiation. These initiations, as I have described to you, can be achieved by any chela or student who wishes to bring their energies into alignment with the greater Plan Divine.

Contained within these Golden Cities, yes indeed, is a higher level of understanding and a higher level of healing and integration of the self. It also allows for the individual to embrace collective consciousness and enter into the great mind of Unana. Dear ones, Dear hearts, when one is readied, shall we say, to enter into the doors of the Temple Supreme, then one is ready to have a greater understanding and a greater spiritual experience. The Golden City Vortices have been brought forward for this great intervention among humanity.

GENETIC MANIPULATION

Yes, there was a time upon your Earth Plane and Planet when the genetic codes were indeed interfered with and this interfering brought back a great shrinking of the Unfed Flame of Love, Wisdom, and Power. I have explained this before in other historical documents. This brought about an encumbrance to the human being…the ability to communicate with plants and with animals then diminished…the ability to communicate and also move at an inter-dimensional level then depleted. For you see Dear ones, Dear hearts, it is through this work that total integration of thought, feeling, and action is brought into that foundation of perfect harmony and perfect balance and one is then able to understand the Fourth and Fifth Dimensional consciousness. This perfect balance has been understood in your world as perfection. It is difficult for the human, in its present condition, to understand this idea of perfection but know Dear one, Dear heart, that perfection lies within. Indeed, this perfection lies within the Eight-sided Cell of Perfection and the Unfed Flame that resides within.

PERFECTION OF THE UNFED FLAME

These teachings that I have brought forward give an understanding of where you are in this present moment. Of course, we entered into that time of Kali Yuga, a time where consciousness would not be fed by the greater light, but instead would be fed by darkness. But at any time, as I have always said, one may overcome the tests of Kali and move into a greater understanding of consciousness. That is why the Prophecies of the Golden Age supreme have always been given. These greater prophecies have been given so you can out-picture to a greater understanding, to a greater consciousness. Beyond Kali Yuga, the time of darkness, lies a time of light. Let us keep our focus upon that time of light. Let us keep our focus upon the perfection in the Unfed Flame within.

This Flame of the Eternal that burns within the heart is beyond the Flame of Desire. It is that great connection to the God-self, to the I AM Presence. This is held also in the genetic codes. Perhaps there has been a great emphasis put upon the manipulation of the genetic codes, for what it does not contain, but let us now talk about what the genetic codes do contain. The genetic codes contain a blueprint for perfection…the genetic codes contain a blueprint for higher understanding…the genetic codes contain a connection to the I AM Presence. This of course is known and accepted and that is why our tradition comes forward to bring forth the growth of this knowledge.

COMMAND THE FLAME

When you call upon the I AM Presence, you command and demand the genetics of your being into action. You command and demand this Unfed Flame to come forward in its greater activity of thought, feeling, and action.

> Beloved mighty I AM Presence,
> come forth in the perfection and balance
> of the Unfed Flame of Love, Wisdom, and Power.
> May this balance prevail throughout my lifestream.
> May this balance bring me forward to the perfection I AM.
> SO BE IT!

Response: *SO BE IT!*

CHOICE AND THE WILL

Let us put the focus then upon the Golden Age. Let us put our focus upon the potential that lies within; for there and only there, will your growth be achieved. Let us put our focus upon the choice that is contained therein. Let us put our focus upon the creation of a new world. Yes, you learn in a turbulent time. Yet, you learn in a time when all possibilities and potentials do exist. That is why we gave you the Teachings of the Six Maps, was it not?

Answer: *Yes.*

Those were brought forward to give the true teaching of prophecy…to give the true teaching of choice…to give the true teaching of the will. The will is also a perfected entity within the genetic code. However, in the collective media, there has been a focus put upon a collective type of consciousness to overtake the little will. But there is this greater will, this greater will that resides within and it too, Dear ones, is connected to the greater I AM.

> Beloved mighty I AM Presence,
> come forth in the Blue Ray of that great Will Divine.
> May my little will align to the greater Will I AM.
> May all that I AM serve the greater Plan
> and Blueprint Divine.
> SO BE IT!

Response: *Hitaka.*

THE SPOKEN WORD

I give you these decrees Dear ones, Dear hearts, so you may begin to understand the power of your spoken word and the power of your thought. Do you not sense, even in the emotion in my voice when I bring these decrees forward, the great force, the great certainty? All of these come forward in that perfect blend, do they not, of thought, feeling, and action? That is why we have given the teaching of the spoken word. That is why we have given the teaching of the decree.

HEALING THROUGH THE TEMPLES OF CONSCIOUSNESS

These spots upon the Earth Plane and Planet seem like little spots indeed when seen from far away but become great ones when you move into these Temples supreme. Not only are these an energy focus of the Earth but also, an energy focus upon the human body, as you have understood for some time. The chakra spin in your own energy centers and the chakra spin on the Earth are known as a Vortex or Vortices. They have been brought forward, not only as protected areas, but areas that would bring great spiritual evolution and teaching to humanity. Each is overseen, as I have stated many times before, by the consciousness eternal, the consciousness and focus of an Ascended Being. They are also assisted by an Elohim and an Archangel. This is to bring forth the continuity and evolution of a Ray Force and bring one into a higher understanding of that Ray Force in its expression in the Fourth and in the Fifth Dimension.

In moving into these other dimensions of light, one then is able to integrate much more, with a resonance with the Unfed Flame and the Eight-sided Cell of Perfection. In moving to the Fourth and Fifth Dimensional awareness of consciousness, this Cell begins to duplicate and the seamless garment is woven again at another level of understanding. This energy adjustment is very important indeed and each of these great Temples of Consciousness comes forward to serve at a greater healing and alignment.

TEMPLE OF GOBEAN

The Temple of Gobean brings forward a greater understanding of the will and brings forward a healing that brings transformation to the soul. One then is able to integrate many of the mistakes of the past and bring them into that greater understanding. In entering the Temple of Gobean, one comes under the tutelage of the Master Teacher El Morya. His work will bring about the consequence of choice. It will bring one to understand how choices are used indeed in Co-creation and it is the consequence of choice that leads us into a temporary action. Now a temporary action is experienced always in the present but a temporary action is always the trigger or charge that begins again another action that will be played out at a future date. So when one begins to understand this focus through the Master Teacher El Morya, one begins to see how choices that are made indeed become immortal. These immortal choices are very, very important Dear ones, Dear hearts, for they are constantly creating. Your constant reaffirmation of choices is the intention of your Co-creation.

It is important, in this Temple of Gobean, to understand this higher understanding of choice and see it at a level of spiritual initiation. One will feel first a tingling in the spine. Is this the activation of the Kundalini? At a certain level indeed it is, but more than that, one will feel the activation of the will chakras, which exist between the shoulders of the back, in the throat area, and upon occasion, also have an influence on the Third Eye Chakra. So you see, Dear ones, Dear heart, the will to do is very important indeed. This statement, "To do, to dare, and to be silent" is trusting in the intention of choice. This is the higher knowledge and initiation of the Temple of Gobean. While I can tell you that such lessons will be brought forward, one will not know them indeed until they have had the experience.

TEMPLE OF MALTON

The Temple of Malton brings about a most wondrous initiation, for there one is able to begin to hear and communicate with the animals and with the plants, as they did in other lifetimes of Atlantis. The vision of the Third Eye is opened and the Kingdom of the fairies, gnomes, and elementals is then opened. What is this Dear ones, Dear hearts, but attainment of the true self. In Malton, the initiation, as once was received in the Temples of Atlantis, brings forward its greater understanding. Of course, one comes under the tutelage of the great teacher Master Kuthumi. One then begins also to understand the great alignment to the sacred geometry of the worlds and how this sacred geometry exists in nature and mirrors itself to all living creation and creatures. This greater attainment brings a fruition to desires, does it not? For then, in understanding how all of elemental life is inter-connected, one then begins to understand the true nature of precipitation…the true nature of manifestation…the true nature of the blend of thought and feeling.

TEMPLE OF WAHANEE

The great Temple and initiation of Wahanee brings forward a greater transmutation and a greater Alchemy, for one then moves from the Fourth Dimension into the Fifth. There one is able to see that greater plan of Divine Brotherhood and Sisterhood and how all hearts are ideally linked as ONE…all lifetimes are linked as one purpose…all is inter-connected in that greater understanding or web of life. The Fifth Dimensional initiation brings one to a greater understanding of the need for Tolerance, Mercy, and Forgiveness of Brothers and Sisters. It brings a greater understanding of that Violet Ray and the work of compassion. These initiations are at times some of the harder initiations, for the Sacred Fire must be called upon and used in vigilance.

The Sacred Fire in the third initiation is most important and this is where many fall back when they hear the call within. Some tremble in entry to the Doors, for what is asked at this level is an understanding beyond the temporal, beyond all illusion; for there, the understanding comes for forgiveness pure and simple and this forgiveness comes first of self and dropping the perception of judgment of self. Our hells and our heavens are created in our thoughts. Our hells and our heavens are the doubt in our actions. This is an initiation brought forward in the Temple of Wahanee. Know Dear one, the information I bring to you is only for one who is desirous to know the great beyond.

TEMPLE OF SHALAHAH

Let us now move to the great Temple of Shalahah. For once one has been tempered through the great fires and the opening of the heart of Wahanee, the fourth initiation is welcomed indeed and your tears are wiped from your face and there, beloved Brother Sananda greets you in joy and says "Om Sheahah. I AM as ONE, Dear one." Enter into the initiation. Enter into the Temple of Healing and Prosperity. In the fourth initiation, one then comes to a greater understanding of prosperity, a greater age, and knowledge for all. One comes to that greater understanding of Unity Consciousness and the healing energy that is contained at any moment. There one knows that statement "I and my Brother, we are as ONE." It brings its completion, for there is that greater understanding that all, beyond the inter-connection, are linked as ONE heart in the Law of Love.

TEMPLE OF KLEHMA

The fifth and the final initiation brings one to the capstone of understanding. It is in Klehma and there, under the watchful tutelage of Serapis Bey, comes forward the Great White Ray of Purification and there again, one does the choosing supreme. One then decides, in that final moment, to release all that comes under the bondage to temporal illusion and enter into the fires of the Ascension. This brings its great reward of Alchemy, Dear ones, Dear hearts, for in these purifying fires comes a greater understanding of Unity Consciousness and total cooperation and harmony for all Brothers and Sisters united as ONE. This cooperation that exists, not only from the Vegetable to the Mineral Kingdom and onward into the Human Kingdom, extends itself onward into other Kingdoms of Creation, of other service systems and other planetary life streams. This is most important to understand Dear ones, Dear hearts, for glimpsing into the five initiations will bring one to a higher consciousness, a cosmic consciousness. Now, Dear one, do you have questions?

EVOLUTION THROUGH THE PERFECT CELL

Question: *Yes. You have spoken of the great Perfected Cell, and you have stated, as far as I understand, that the Unfed Flame burns inside that cell. Did I understand that correctly?*

It is correct Dear one. It is seen in the third and fourth layers of the energy fields. It is seen at a light energy level. Of course, it is important to understand that this is a genetic that is encoded and was never interfered with, was never allowed to be interfered with.

Question: *So what you are saying, at a genetic level, is that the coding that has been altered can be reversed by the use of the Violet Flame?*

What I am saying Dear ones, Dear hearts, is the decrees that I have given to you today will foster and support the growth of the Unfed Flame and the perfection within. It is only natural, is it not, for a seed, when it is planted in healthy and virile soil and watered, that it will sprout? Will it not then take root and soon a plant, a true little seedling, will grow and from there, soon a tree evolves? This is the process, is it not, as mirrored in your natural universe?

Question: *Yes it is. Then these decrees that you have given today will aid and foster this evolutionary process?*

Indeed, Dear one.

CHAKRAS AND THE FIVE GOLDEN CITIES

Question: *As far as the initiations for each of the Golden Cities, am I correct in assuming that in the Golden Age, people will migrate from city to city as their evolution demands?*

This is the ideal purpose of these locations. Now to clarify, I would also like to give you corresponding Chakra Centers, so those who have the eyes to see and ears to hear will also understand. I have given you the Chakra Centers as they correlate to Gobean. For Malton, the Chakra Centers are indeed the Pineal, or the Third Eye Chakra, and also the Base, or Root Chakra. These are the two that are first felt in their opening in this Golden City Vortex. Now, when entering into Wahanee, there is an opening of the Heart Chakra alongside an opening of the Throat Chakra. When one enters into Shalahah, one feels a greater opening with the Solar Plexus and Crown Chakra, and also again, with the Throat Chakra. And with the Ascension, or shall we say, the Klehma Vortex, it is very important to understand that it is a complete opening of the Sexual Chakra alongside an opening of the Crown Chakra. [See Appendix E, *Chakras and the Five United States Golden Cities.*]

Question: *That is most interesting. Is the opening of the chakras at all layers, at all levels of development?*

It is an opening of these chakras at Fourth and Fifth Dimensional consciousness. I am not speaking of a Third Dimensional consciousness.

Response: *I see. I understand.*

I am speaking at a higher level of understanding.

TEMPLES OF EVOLUTION AND LIGHT

Response and question: *I see. I understand what you're saying. In moving on to the initiation process, is there an optimum time for an individual to spend in each of the Golden Cities or is it on an-as-needed basis and this could continue on for more than one lifetime, couldn't it?*

One is drawn as they hear the message within. It is always best to receive that message from within. When the student is ready, the Master appears. But it is true, one may travel through the initiations through several successive lifetimes; however, one would achieve great acceleration through moving through all five successively and also opening to the higher understanding of these initiatory rights.

Question: *Yes, I think I understand what you are saying. It would be a step-by-step progression for an individual to do so. In understanding the Golden Cities, are they Temples for our evolution and transmutation?*

Indeed Dear ones, Dear hearts, they have been brought forth for all states that may be created in this prophetic time. If indeed humanity experiences a time of tumultuous change through the Earth Changes and geophysical change, then these areas will bring about a preservation or a protection of the higher spiritual truths and understandings. If humanity chooses to take the higher road and listens to the message of the prophets, listens to the message that is contained in the prophecies, then these areas will serve to bring humanity into a greater evolution and alignment with the light of the Central Sun.

Question: *So, what you are saying is that at one level these Golden Cities are the future population centers and at another level, they are a step-by-step progression to free the spirit?*

It is true, Dear one. So one may then enter into that seamless garment. One may then enter into their Ascension.

Response: *I see. It makes perfect sense. At this moment I have no further questions with regard to the information that you have brought forward today.*

SO BE IT! Dear one, in light and understanding of the greater, I AM Saint Germain.

Response: *Thank you very much.*

6

True Memory
Saint Germain

Greetings Beloved chelas in that mighty Violet Fire. I AM Saint Germain and I stream forth on that Violet Ray of Mercy, Compassion, and ultimate Forgiveness. As usual Dear hearts, I request permission to come forward.

Response: *Please Saint Germain, you are most welcome, come forward.*

There is still much work for us to complete Dear ones, Dear hearts, and I remind you always to call upon that mighty Violet Flame to bring you forward in this work. If you feel an obstruction in front of you, something that is blocking your way, your vision, or your mind, set your heart upon that mighty Violet Flame. Call it forward and there, Dear ones, is indeed that most refreshing drink that will give you the impetus to complete. Have courage Dear ones, Dear hearts, in this great Time of Testing. Have courage and move forward.

TIME AND ILLUSION

Today Dear ones, Dear hearts, I should like to continue a discourse that I have brought forward many times before but I feel it is important to bring it forward again. It is indeed always a new perspective that will lend another inspiration or idea to bring forth a completion. Memory is part of the work of conscious immortality. As I have always said, immortality is comprised first of that consciousness.

Conscious immortality arise! There is the deathless and true seamless garment, the seamless body of light. Dear ones, Dear hearts, when we speak of memory, we speak of all the experiences that have been collected throughout the barrier of time. I say "the barrier of time," for time is the ultimate of all illusions.

Man moves every day according to a clock. His impressions are based upon the time of the present moment…upon the time of the past…upon the pressures of the future. Dear ones, Dear hearts, you see with time, we enter into the grandest of all illusions and yet time becomes the greatest of all teachers. The body, as it travels through time, takes on, shall we say, each well-earned line. The body ages according to the perception of time, for each person has their own idea or perception of what time is within the illusion. See for yourself in your own experience. Look at yourself in your own perception and you will see that time comes to you from your own mind. So, is this indeed a group of minds that are collectively choosing to learn through the illusion of time? It is very possible Dear ones, Dear hearts. But let us address the memory and how memory plays its own illusion within time.

MIND, CHOICE, ACTION, AND MEMORY

Mind, Dear ones, Dear hearts, is indeed as you have always known, the ultimate of all builders, for mind is the thought that brings forward the grand architect of action. Emotion of course bridges the thought into the grand action. So mind is comprised, not only of intentions and choices which comprise the will, but also a complete and total archive and at times a factory of memory. Memory contains many experiences, yes, that have shaped your personality and shaped each action and subsequent thought. Memory contains within it, not only the actual archive of these actions, but also your perceptions or senses enacting with each action. These sensations, feelings, or perceptions of a situation change completely over time.

Memories that you hold of the past may not indeed be exactly the same as the action when you were within it. Many people understand this, therefore they carry with them only fond memories of the past and choose to forget any situation that had caused them pain or any trouble.

Dear ones, Dear hearts, the troubling aspects of the self are often dropped off to the side and ignored and the positive aspects are then brought forward. This is true of human nature and that may serve the incarnation well. This brings a strict justification to the present to engender more choices through that filter of positive experiences. It leads one to a greater understanding and to even drop the idea of memory.

INHIBITING PERCEPTIONS OF SELF

Memory brings forward a perception of history, a perception of past experience. But memory, in order to enter into an all-encompassing consciousness of the ONE, must be detached. This of course is a painful experience for those who are so attached to their memories and the idea that it was a certain way. It is important to understand that this detachment process from memory should not disallow the past, not disallow the foundation which you see as yourself, but instead allow you to enter into your pure divinity and be able then to enter into a world that exists beyond inhibiting self-perception.

It is important to understand Dear ones, Dear hearts, that the self does inhibit itself so many times from bringing forward its true divinity, its true God I AM. The God I AM exists beyond time. The God I AM exists beyond memory. The God I AM exists beyond all limitation. The God I AM exists in the now, into an ever-present now. This all-encompassing presence of God is the all-knowing perfection and encompasses all divinity. Dear ones, Dear hearts, of course it is at times almost impossible to perceive that you could exist without a memory of the past; however, let us look at an example so you may learn even more deeply.

SURRENDER JUDGMENTS

It is not that you forget the past but that you detach from the past. Memories of the past no longer provoke within you a sensation that is good or a sensation that is bad. It is brought to the understanding that all was experience, to serve the ever present now. This of course is sometimes very difficult for the human to understand because indeed it embraces the all-encompassing immortality of the soul. Even today, there are actions that occur within your life that are related to past life experiences. These actions, as they are brought forward, as they are well intended to do, provoke again an opportunity for how you shall surrender judgment. This surrendering of judgment is the release of good versus bad, of light versus dark, of evil versus righteousness.

Dear ones, Dear hearts, these little charges that are positive or negative in their influence, then create yet another action upon the timeline of the soul. The soul then becomes captured within that field of time, working for a way to free itself from the bondage of memory. Memory holds within it, not only these sensations or feelings that bridge thoughts and actions together into the ultimate field of maya or illusion, they also hold within them many codes of genetics. These genetic codes are also activated through certain sensations within the human aura itself. This DNA coding which holds the genetic code keeps you bound to this plane of unreality. We have spoken of this so many times before, the simplicity of the spiritual law is about whether one is choosing fear versus the ultimate choice of love.

FREEDOM THROUGH LOVE

It is ever so difficult to move away from the encoding of fear, ever so difficult to move away from the path that one has always traveled. But know this Dear ones, Dear hearts, in embracing the all-encompassing Law of Love, one then moves into a new understanding. It prepares the soul to move into the boundlessness of conscious immortality. There the mind is freed. The mind then bridges into action and complete freedom. As I have always said "Down with death. Conscious immortality arise!"

EXPERIENCE THE GOD-MAN

Dear ones, Dear hearts, this conscious immortality embraces the True Memory. Now let us speak of True Memory. True Memory vibrates with the resonance of the Divine God-man that resides within each and every one of you. True Memory recognizes that there is no limitation placed through time, that all is happening simultaneously. As I have pointed out to you before in the point of perception, that at this moment, you are only thinking in this present time experience but there are other time experiences of you that are still existing and experiencing simultaneously. In this moment of you is the memory and the perception of twenty years ago, thirty years ago, twenty years from now, thirty years from now. In that radial experience of understanding time, you see that you are so much more beyond the experience of just this one present moment. The true experience of knowing the God-man, knows that all time happens simultaneously and all time happens for one reason: to educate the soul and bring it into higher awareness of its true self... higher awareness of its true capability...higher awareness of its true potential.

THE PLEASANT PRISON

The use of the Violet Flame allows the chela to bring this awareness into a greater capacity. Dear ones, Dear hearts, the use of the Violet Flame allows you to transmute positive or negative charges. Now, it is probably hard to see a positive experience as an encumbrance that keeps one from eternal freedom but when one has a pleasant surrounding in the prison of the mind, how would one ever want to leave? Having the best food in the prison of the mind, why would one then want to escape? One is then content and happy and has created, through the lower form of desires, their own entrapment.

EXPANSION THROUGH EXPERIENCE

Now remember Dear ones, Dear hearts, that when I speak of desires, there are indeed the higher teachings on the desire of the Source. "Of the Source" is much misinterpreted. This means "of the God-man," the higher nature that exists within the human. The human is evolving through this understanding of memory and this evolvement allows then for a greater development of the will to choose an experience. To see that an experience contains both negative and positive charges, one can then detach from the experience and see the growth that was achieved. This growth leads always to the eternal ONE, to the heart of love. As it has always been said, "When all is said and done, what is left Dear ones, but that mighty Law of Love." Then one sees the expansion of the true heart. One then sees the expansion of the true spirit of humanity.

BLISS OR PAIN?

Dear ones, memory has been brought forward as a great teacher but consider this, that memory can be chosen. Memory that is held can always be returned to and understood from a fresh perspective.

It is important to understand memory, for memory plays such an extensive role in the choices that you are making, even in this moment. The memory of pains that you have had in the past may keep you from making a choice today, in this moment, of how you shall travel the spiritual path. A memory of bliss, a memory of happiness, may also then push you along the path in a certain manner and in a certain way. But what if neither of the memories existed?

What if the path of pain or the path of pleasure did not exist at all? Where would that take you Dear one, Dear chela? It would take you to the center of your being...it would take you beyond strife... it would take you beyond the push...it would take you beyond the pull to the center of your being. There you would return and you would see the all-encompassing love that is the force behind all activity. You would then see this greater existence of mind. You would then see the greater existence of action. It is much to fathom Dear ones, Dear hearts, but it is indeed another factor and critical key in understanding the immortality of consciousness.

INTERCONNECTED

It is said that a fool is often soon parted from his money. Why is that so? Because of a past experience, the past experience being the memory that he carries. Now what if the fool no longer saw himself as the fool? Would he then be so quickly parted? He would have a new perception, a new understanding that came from the detachment of memory. The detachment of memory allows then a greater understanding. This greater understanding of the archive of the soul then moves forward into understanding the true self, the God-man, the HU-man. All works for the betterment of the ONE. This indeed is a universal law. All does not work for the betterment of the individual but all works for the betterment of the soul and that soul is interconnected into a greater harmony, into a greater ONE.

It is hard to understand in one individual embodiment, why one person would have such pain and another would have such pleasure but that is viewing life from a very narrow perspective, a narrow perspective of only one given moment. When all is embraced in a greater understanding, into a greater detachment of the archive of memory, one then begins to understand, in its greater glory, the interconnectedness of all of life. Each moment we experience history and even in this moment, is this not history creating itself? Isn't it just a perception of experience that makes it either negative or positive? Do you remember Dear ones, Dear heart, when Sananda gave the teaching of the open door? He was speaking of opening the mind.

MEMORY, CHOICE, AND NATURAL SELECTION

To see an experience as not just one thing and to see the opportunity for many, many perceptions within that experience, there the memory can become encoded in many different ways. This memory plays a role in the creation of genetics. This is a type of natural selection, where the mind plays a natural role in selection and bridges with emotion, feeling, and sensation into the action world, where the creation comes forth. This natural selection, yes, plays a role in engendering the will, but let us speak about liberation. Let us keep our focus upon the end result. This is the Ascension of consciousness in its own timing, each door opening successively for its Purpose Divine.

DETACHMENT AND LOVE

This is why Dear ones, Dear hearts, we have given the sacred instruction on the Violet Fire and how to invoke its use. For you see, of all the keys that we have given you, the use of the sacred Violet Fire is indeed the one where you shall find your eternal freedom. It creates an opportunity to detach from decided memories. Then memory is seen as neither a negative or positive experience. It is seen with a greater vision, a greater scope, and with hope and wonder for creation. This is why we have given dietary requirements, for now you understand that the eating of flesh indeed brings you only to one experience, to one perception of consciousness. That is why the Master Teacher very often brings forward the greater disciplines, to bring you into a greater understanding of the polar opposites that exist together in one situation. This brings about a complete conditioning of the mind.

If your mind is only conditioned to see something so far, you will only see it so far. But the Master Teacher brings forward a different condition, so you may see something in a new and unique way. Memory carries, as I have said before, this great archive of experiences. The Violet Flame helps the soul to understand this archive of experiences with complete detachment, to move always into the one eternal law, the Law of Love. Questions?

OVERSOUL

Question: *Yes. True memory is relational to divinity in all things, is it not?*

It is, Dear one.

Question: *And so the great oversoul, do all Divine Sparks stream from that?*

Dear one, Dear heart, there is no limitation upon creation and levels of understanding of consciousness. The inter-connectivity of life takes on a broader and even more wondrous understanding. But, as it has always been said before, let us take little steps into this understanding. Indeed, there are oversouls. These oversouls provide that great connection that one soul may feel with another. The pulsation of this oversoul is the connection of not smaller but individualized experiences. It is important to not see the concept of the oversoul in a hierarchical manner but instead, to see it as a more specialized understanding. The oversoul functions in this way: it sends out individual life streams to have more specialized experience. Indeed, there is a connection between all of humanity. Indeed, we are as ONE.

BEYOND ILLUSION

Question: *So since humanity is as ONE, then the I AM Presence, is there only one?*

Ultimately, in the greater and grander scheme, there is but one consciousness. This one consciousness fills and permeates all of life but it is very difficult, even in our day-to-day life, to understand this one consciousness. There are those who have the eyes to see and the ears to hear that know there is an inter-connectivity existing beyond the physical. The physical experience is given so one may see the limitation that can be placed at times through consciousness. The physical is also given so that consciousness can be seen on the other side without limit. The spiritual experience permeates all of the physical and yet it connects seamlessly and timelessly beyond all illusion. There is the great, unified ONE. Questions?

EXPERIENCE THE TRUE SELF

Question: *Yes. By accepting that all memories are just experience, to give the individual a greater understanding of creation and the elements of choice, then the retaining of fond memories and the forgetting of unfond memories is no longer necessary?*

It is not a forgetting. Instead Dear ones, Dear hearts, it is remembrance of me, I AM. It is remembrance of the true self. That is the reason for the element of detachment, to see that it was just experience, experience given to bring you to a higher understanding…a higher awareness…a greater and a deeper unity…that unity based upon the Law of Love. SO BE IT!

SOUL KNOWS ALL

Response: *SO BE IT! So in that Law of Love, one can accept all experiences as just experience.*

The Law of Love is first given to the self. This is also the concept of At-ONE-Ment, or complete forgiveness of self. For you see, memories of pleasure and pain are completely memories of judgment of self…judgment of experience…judgment of actions taken for good or for bad. This judgment encumbers the soul. When understood at the level of the great remembrance of I AM, then one sees all elements at play in memory. This memory carries indeed the genetic form. It carries indeed the body that dies. But inside the body that dies is the soul that knows all. When you touch into the heart of the great I AM, you then encounter the soul that knows all, that is in touch with the universal archive of All That Is. This universal archive is beyond the individual archive. It contains all knowing, all knowledge. It has been referred to at times as Akasha. But indeed, Dear ones, Dear hearts, it is known only as the ONE, for it shows the inter-connectivity of all thought, all feeling, and all action.

FOUNTAIN OF YOUTH

It is important to understand and embrace a diversity of experience. It is important to not leave experience until one is ready to do so. But when one sees the many tears…the many laughs…the many disappointments…the many joys, then one is able to embrace the all-ness of life. This Oneness of life is the ever-present fountain of youth. This fountain of youth embraces life eternal, without judgment, and knows that within its cycle of change is the cycle of the ever-present now. It embraces all aspects that can exist within the cycles of change. Life then becomes the most refreshing drink. Questions?

A DEVELOPED MEMORY

Question: *Yes. Then for those who have practiced immortality in this dimensional realm, their memory is quite extensive and developed, is it not?*

The memory becomes so developed, it can recall at any given time, any lifetime of experience. But this memory is developed with great compassion and detachment of self. This compassion is necessary, so that judgment of self does not occur; for it is in the judgment of self that a negative or positive charge then occurs. One sees the self as wrong; one sees the self as righteous. Do these not inhibit the soul in seeing the truer picture and the connection of all as ONE?

Resonse: *Yes they do.*

This greater tolerance calls for a greater heart, calls for a greater understanding. But until one is readied, as it has been said, when the heart opens and the feet are washed in the blood of the heart, one is not yet ready to meet the true Master. But when this does indeed happen, one then understands a love that moves beyond the self. It is a love that binds all together as one eternal force. Questions?

FORGIVENESS AND NATURAL LAW

Response: *Yes. The concepts of compassion and detachment sometimes almost seem paradoxical or at odds with each other, yet both are needed to release the difficult judgment of the self.*

It is hard, Dear ones, for you see within illusion that there are many placed in your lifetimes to serve as mirrors of the mighty law existing within yourself. These mirrors come forward in many different aspects. They come forward to show many positive experiences and many negative experiences but compassion is developed. That is why, when using the Violet Flame, you build an understanding of compassion. Compassion begins with forgiveness of self. Now when this is stated, it is understood with a clarity for natural law. Nature forgives itself. Look at this all the time. Do plants hold grudges? Do animals offer forgiveness for who and what they are? You see Dear ones, Dear hearts, even within the Mineral Kingdom, these natural laws reveal and show themselves to you.

AWAKENING

The human is more complex, for humans allow social situations to deem their worthiness. They rely upon money to see if they made the right choice or the wrong choice. They rely upon material reflection and status in the society to say, "I have done the right thing, haven't I?" These questions are produced and mirrored out to the culture and the society that the soul has chosen as an experience. But then there is that moment, is there not, of awakening? The moment of seeing this nonsense with great humor, great tears, and great laughter, one then chooses again a greater opening. This is indeed the open door. Questions?

COMPASSION, MERCY, FREEDOM

Response: *At some point, I know we will all free ourselves from this and move onward. At what time this is, I don't know.*

Know that the Violet Flame is the great liberator, Dear ones, Dear hearts. There is no greater law that is for you. There is no Master Teacher that can free you but yourself and your own application of these laws eternal. Compassion, develop it, Dear ones. Mercy, understand it completely. Freedom, it is your Divine Birthright. SO BE IT!

Response: *SO BE IT! At this moment I have no further questions for this discourse.*

In that mighty Christ, I AM Saint Germain.

7

Ascension through the Dimensions
Saint Germain

Greetings my Beloved chelas in that mighty Christ. I AM Saint Germain and I stream forth on that Violet Ray of Mercy, Compassion, and Forgiveness. As usual Dear hearts, I request permission to come forward?

Response: *Please Saint Germain, you are most welcome and please come forward.*

THE SPIRITUAL TRAINING OF THE MIND

There is much work still for us to complete, is there not Dear ones, Dear hearts? Much work for us to complete upon this Earth Plane and Planet. You see Dear ones, we have brought forward the work of Earth Changes Prophecy to reflect the work that is to be done with the planet, that work held in the sacred stewardship for beloved Babajeran. But there is also that work held within that sacred stewardship of the Ascended Masters. That is the work for humanity, for it to gain in understanding, not only at a spiritual level but also at other levels of the mind. The training of the mind will bring it into complete alignment with its own feeling world. This alignment of thought, feeling, and action is understood, not only in your own world, but also extends on into more subtle understandings within the Fourth and Fifth Dimension.

ASCENSION OF SOULS

The process of extending this understanding and how it reflects into your inner world is the process of Ascension. This Ascension process correlates with the changes of the planet herself. For you see Dear ones, Dear hearts, it is a great graduation of souls . . . it is a great ascent . . . it is a great Rapture. This great Rapture, or Ascension of souls, has been brought forward within its own timing and pure intention. This intention of course was determined long ago but the soul, in its sojourn, is now ready to move forward. A great completion is ready. As Dear Sananda has always said to you Dear ones, Dear chelas of my heart, "The minutes and the seconds tick. The time is at hand. The time has come for man to receive the gift." This gift is the gift of Ascension.

THE OPEN HEART

These higher teachings, as you are ready to understand, as the eyes and the ears are open, come forward to bring you into that process of Ascension. Of course, we also bring this into an alignment with the other densities . . . the alignment of the body . . . the alignment of the mind . . . the alignment of the spirit. All of these come together in their great timing and also intention. For the body, we have given a great focus upon the work of the diet. We give great focus upon the healing of the body; that is, that greater alignment again of the mind, body, and spirit. This always works through that open heart, does it not? For within that open heart, one is then willing to receive healing at an even greater level. It is this opening of the heart that is ever so important in the understanding of this work and preparing the chela to understand the Fourth Dimension and to open a glimpse into a Fifth Dimensional reality.

AN EXPONENTIAL LEAP

As you see Dear ones, light in its own separation shows the differences that you experience as color. You also know, within this range of understanding, that sound separates as well, giving different tones or qualities. This same experience is within the Third Dimension. The same experience is in within the Fourth Dimension. The same experience is in within the Fifth Dimension. But it is important to understand, as we move through one dimension, or octave, to the next, there is indeed an exponential leap in this range of understanding. So again, let me explain this through a chart.

We will start again with the Third Dimension and let us deal now only in the Third Dimension with seven harmonics of understanding. Do you see this chart?

Response: *Yes.*

This first level represents the Third Dimension and its seven harmonics of colors and sounds. This is the experience brought through the five senses of touch, smell, hearing, sight, and taste. Moving onto the Fourth Dimension, we move in an exponential ratio, moving from seven harmonics to fourteen harmonics. This comprises the Fourth Dimension. Moving onto the Fifth Dimension, we would have again an exponential, to a twenty-eight degree harmonic. This may give you some understanding when relating mathematically to the Third, Fourth, and Fifth Dimensions.

[*This chart show seven, fourteen, and twenty-eight frequencies, quite distinguishable and visible. Seven are functioning at the Third Dimensional level, fourteen at the Fourth, and twenty-eight at the Fifth.*]

ENERGY FIELDS OF THE FOURTH DIMENSION

Many people are of the opinion that the move into the Fourth Dimension, or making that leap of the octave, they are then moving into an eighth, ninth, or tenth layer of the existing field of the Third Dimension. This is not true, Dear ones, Dear hearts. While there are expansions of experiences within the Third Dimension, there is that great deciding moment—a defining moment—which can be felt when you move between the octaves. This is the same as when a sound barrier is broken or when a light barrier is broken and is as thin a barrier that has then broken. In the moment that I come forward for instruction, do you not hear, at the inner level, a barrier that is being broken?

Response: *I can hear the pitch open up as you step through.*

This barrier, as I am now defining for you, is indeed that fine moment that exists between the Third and the Fourth Dimension. Now it has always been your opinion that when I come forward to bring discourse, I am projecting my energy through the Fifth Dimension, through the Fourth Dimension, and onward; but we are speaking of consciousness, consciousness as thought. These thoughts permeate from the Fifth Dimension to the Fourth Dimensional understanding. There they move again, as I have stated, through fourteen levels of differentiation. From there, they move onward into the level where they are embraced through the human senses.

A RANGE OF RAY FORCES

Now, to bring this into a greater understanding: a molecule exists and is protected through the physical structure of the neutron, the proton, and the electron; these physical structures allow mass and matter to exist in your physical world. Similarly, if the consciousness were to move from a different understanding through the Fifth, to the Fourth, and onward to the Third Dimension, there would be the elemental life force which would come forward and bring great service in that motion. You have understood the elemental life force and how it exists on your planet only at a primary level, relating to wind, water, earth, and fire. These primary elements are of course an expression of a higher force that exists from the Fourth Dimension. Again, as you hear these words, known to you in a clairaudient manner, are they not indeed words that come from the Fifth Dimension, arcing through this Fourth Dimensional range of Ray Forces, and moving again into another range of Ray Forces? Questions?

Response: *Lots of questions.*

WHEN THE TIME IS RIGHT

I shall proceed first. Perhaps in this second part of this discussion, I can shed even greater light and greater sound upon the purpose and the reason for this instruction.

The Golden City Vortices exist in their own timing and intention. I say this very often, "timing and intention." It is important always that one is not led too early for that drink, for is it then truly appreciated? One should never be forced beyond their time to learn something they are not ready yet to learn. We start always in beginning steps and are led one step after another into a greater understanding.

The heart cannot be opened immediately, not until the lessons of true love, true compassion, and true mercy can be learned. These of course always come as lessons of the heart, lessons that come in their timing and in their intention. But until those lessons are learned, one is not readied. One is not ready yet to understand a greater instruction. But intention can always be held in its purity. Intention can always be held to bring forward that greater lesson . . . to bring forward that greater Light Divine . . . to bring forward that greater sound, which is indeed the song of God. Intention then is qualified through the proper timing. One then knows that when the time is right, the intention flows forward and all moves with that greater harmony of which I speak. Now, I shall continue on this understanding.

BABAJERAN AND THE ELEMENTAL LIFE FORCE

The great Earth Changes are coming forward to bring a great purification. This has always been known by those who have the eyes to see and the ears to hear. What were they seeing? What were they listening to? But to the inner kingdoms of the Fourth Dimension that are, were, and always shall be. These inner kingdoms exist Dear ones, Dear hearts, bringing their service in even a greater degree to beloved Babajeran. They know the purpose of her heart, the purpose of her mind, and the purpose of her greater will. Of course, it is always difficult for one who comes from a Third Dimensional understanding, which sees the Earth only as a forest . . . only as a mountain . . . only as a river . . . only as a strata to be conquered. Here lies this mineral; here lies the oil; here lies the coal to be burnt. From the Third Dimensional understanding, the Earth is seen as something to be Mastered, something to be conquered, and something to be understood only through the five senses.

At the Fourth Dimensional level comes a greater understanding. There is a wonderment of creation and of the kingdoms that lie within. Have you ever wondered about the telepathic responses of the Animal Kingdom, their inner connection with nature itself? The songs of the birds, how are they interconnected to the life on Earth and who rides upon their wings? Those who have the eyes to see and the ears to hear know and understand the great service these kingdoms bring forward, this great service of the Elemental Life Force.

THE DIVINE ONESHIP OF NATURE

In entering a Golden City Vortex, one begins this deeper communication, this deeper communion that exists with these kingdoms. This is the ascent of consciousness. This is the ascent of emotion. This is the ascent of higher activity. When one is led naturally to this understanding, they seek the demonstration of natural law. I have given you this understanding of natural law, for within you exists that first Divine Oneship of nature. This indeed is the Eight-sided Cell of Perfection and it is through this Eight-sided Cell of Perfection that you are indeed connected at the Third Dimension, at the Fourth Dimension, and onward to the Fifth Dimension of consciousness. It is this perfected Cell that lies within you, that brings the stream of consciousness forward . . . which becomes that force within that leads you to seek greater harmony, greater divinity, and acceptance of perfection.

OPENING THE DIVINE CELL

The Fourth Dimension is always connected within you, Dear ones, Dear hearts. Through this collective forgetting, understood as the time of Kali Yuga, consciousness has fallen and no longer opens this Cell within at will. But all communion that exists with the Fourth Dimension exists through the opening of this Divine Cell. That is why the work of the Violet Flame has been brought forward at this time. Through calling and invoking its presence, you then begin to understand those great lessons of love . . . those great lessons of compassion . . . those great lessons of mercy and their ever importance in the opening of your heart.

This opening of your heart is not only the opening of the Heart Chakra; it is the opening of this Divine Cell that is connected through these laws of nature to the kingdoms within. These kingdoms that exist in the elementals . . . these kingdoms that exist in the salamanders . . . these kingdoms that exist within the undines . .

. these kingdoms that exist between the gnomes and the fairies, they are indeed at a level that knows and understands a greater harmony. They know and understand the great balancing effect that must take place to keep the Earth in its perfected order.

CHANGE AND CHOICE

Now, Dear ones, Dear hearts, this perfected order also includes change. Change allows for a great cleansing to occur, not only a cleansing of what is not wanted, but also a choosing of what is to be kept. Each time you enter a closet ready to clean, discard, and get rid of what is no longer wanted, in that moment, you will also choose what you will keep . . . you will also choose what you value . . . you will choose what is useful to you. In this Time of Great Change, where humanity and beloved Babajeran are bonded in one natural law through the Fourth Dimension, there is a great assistance that is being given by these beloved beings of light, sound, and their fourteen spaces . . . fourteen directions . . . fourteen understandings of balance. This balance brings itself forward Dear ones, Dear heart, to serve a greater Cause Divine.

INTERCONNECTIVITY

In the Golden Cities, there is a great interaction with these kingdoms. For this communing to occur, for this greater harmonization to come forward, one needs to understand its greater service. It is there to serve the greater heart of desire with another way of approaching and understanding. Conscious immortality is indeed the tie that binds all of these dimensions together; for you see, in conscious immortality, you are able to move beyond a barrier or differentiation. You are able to see the interconnectivity of all of life. You are able then to see the Third Dimension, the Fourth Dimension, and the Fifth Dimension existing, not in a hierarchical sense, but existing in their great spiral of life. Now, I shall open the floor for your questions.

SOUND FREQUENCIES

Question: *Yes. The resonance or sound frequencies between the dimensions, is this where one grouping of sound frequencies start and another grouping stops?*

This is so, Dear one.

Question: *These resonances are the pathways with which the light structures are put forward and sent?*

It is true, Dear one. From the Great Central Sun, they come under a grander direction. A direction is then chosen for Third Dimension. A direction then is orchestrated for Fourth Dimension. This direction at the Fifth Dimension is chosen.

PERCEPTION

Question: *I see. In our world, where the atomic structure is electrons, protons, and neutrons and each one of those is relative to a light ray, to move into the Fourth Dimension, must we have another light Ray? And into the Fifth, we must have yet another light Ray?*

It is not a matter of another light Ray that brings expansion to an understanding of a dimension. It is an orchestration of the light Rays in the Fourth Dimension and complete understanding of these light Rays in the Fifth Dimension. Do you understand? It has to do again with perception. It is the way that light is understood. It is the way that sound is understood. In this moment, the light and sound Ray of my thought, coming to you, is beyond an understanding within the physical and yet a physical demonstration is now being given to you, is it not?

Answer: *You are standing there.*

This perception is of utmost importance. It is important to understand that perception, within itself, is another key in understanding what we would perceive in this moment for this teaching, which is a separation between Third Dimension and Fourth Dimension and a separation between Fourth Dimension and Fifth Dimension. Questions?

Response: *And yet you are still standing there.*

So you see, your perception is one where you have the eyes to see and the ears to hear. But your eyes do indeed still see. Your ears do indeed still hear. They are still one in the same and yet they have been developed to understand at another level, or better yet, along the greater spiral of consciousness. The teaching I bring to you this moment pierces through each of these layers of separation perceived through the limiting Third Dimensional understanding of the five senses. But if one expands the senses, taste can be taken to other levels, can it not?

Answer: *Yes it can.*

Touch can be taken to other levels, can it not?

Answer: *Absolutely.*

This same paradigm can be applied to all of the senses. In this moment, between my words, do you perceive the Great Silence?

Answer: *Of course.*

In this moment, within my words, do you hear another high-pitched ring?

Answer: *Yes.*

This is my point Dear one, Dear heart. All dimensions bring their demonstration of the mighty Truth Divine.

DIVINE CHAMBER OF THE HEART

Question: *And this is accomplished with the opening of the Eight-sided Cell of Perfection?*

The opening indeed, Dear one, of that Divine Chamber of the heart.

Response: *It has been my understanding that it was only through that undeniable sense of love for you and other members of the Spiritual Hierarchy, for the planet, and for humanity, that the Cell would open.*

And so I say, "love will move a mountain," will it not?

Answer: *Yes it will.*

Questions?

Question: *I've noticed that when thought, feeling, and action are completely aligned, that the Ray Forces then open. As you come through, may one pass into that Fourth Dimension with that alignment?*

THE ASCENSION PROCESS AND THE MASTER TEACHER

It is so, Dear one. This indeed is the process of Ascension. It is the process of ascending perception, this perception not to be limited to one definition of the senses. Questions?

Response: *Yes. In aligning the senses, it seems all too easy to focus in different directions at one time, instead of staying on one focus and one intention to create a specific outcome.*

This is the work of the Master Teacher, you see. The Master Teacher comes forward and allows the chela the opportunity to bring a great focus into a certain area and there the gates of freedom are found. Questions?

Response: *At this point, I have no further questions with regard to this particular topic. This will be much for everyone to contemplate.*

Mighty Violet Ray stream forth from the Fifth Dimension
into the hearts of men and women.
May the Fourth Dimension bring its alignment
for greater purification of the Earth Divine.
May all align and Ascend in thy flame.

I AM Saint Germain.

Response: *Thank you very much.*

8

The Heart of Peace
Saint Germain
Sananda

Greetings beloved chelas in that mighty Violet Flame. I AM Saint Germain and I stream forth on that mighty Violet Flame of Mercy, Transmutation, and ultimate Forgiveness. I ask permission to come forward Dear ones, Dear hearts.

Response: *Please Saint Germain come forward. You are most welcome.*

This day I stream forth on that mighty Violet Ray. But today, that Mighty Blue Flame also assists this discourse. The Blue Flame of the Will of God, that streams forth through the heart of the Mighty Logos, the heart of the Great Central Sun. Dear ones, Dear heart, there is much more still for us to continue with our work, much teaching still to impart.

MAKING SENSE OUT OF THE SENSELESS

But I know Dear one, with the current events upon the world scene, there are many whose hearts are very heavy, who wonder at this time how can we make much sense from these situations? But know Dear ones, Dear hearts of mine, those who follow these teachings, that all streams forth in accordance to the Divine Plan and the Divine Will. At times it is impossible to understand the meaning of such events. Sometimes, one may wonder, "How could this serve the Greater Will? How could this be in alignment to any Divine Plan?" Those who are faced with such sorrow…those who are faced with the rebuilding…those who are faced with such fears of the unknown, know this Dear one, Dear heart, that there is no mistake ever, ever, ever. And I repeat this lesson again to you, that all streams forth in a Divine Plan and in a Divine Will.

What I am speaking of is not only that law that exists in all of duality but also that law that is understood as balance. All comes forward seeking a balance. This you have always known. This I have always taught to you. It comes forward, as you would know, in Hermetic Law, in that Law of Rhythm. One side swings to the next; all extremes find their other complement; all seek to find balance in any given situation. You know Dear one, Dear heart, you can only attract unto yourself that which would seek the same vibration. Understand and know this higher law and you will then begin to know and understand the forces that are at work. In this moment, at this moment, you can only attract unto yourself, that which is a like vibration. That is why Dear ones, we have given you the work of the Violet Flame. Call upon that mighty law, that will in action.

> Violet Flame come forth. Stream forth into my will.
> Align my will to the Divine Plan.
> Bring balance to this situation.

TIME OF TESTING

In that moment you call that Violet Flame to bring forth its mighty will in action, the Violet Flame comes forth transmuting and alchemizing any given situation. Yes indeed, as I have stated before, the Violet Flame brings karma, or shall we say, those actions to be understood at a new level, to be understood in a new context. It is important at this time to continue your vigilant use of the Violet Flame, along with the Tube of Light. For you see, I stated some time ago that this would be indeed a Time of Testing. We, at that time, also talked about the end of the Time of Transition. This, of course, was given in accordance to an understanding of the Laws of Prophecy and how prophecy can be used to reach a greater Co-creation alongside the Divine Plan and the Divine Will.

You have well known that prophecy is always given to bring forth a greater change that aligns to a greater harmony. In this context, know and understand that a test is only given to a student when the student is ready. It is not given as a punishment; it is not given to see "Is this person right? Is this person wrong?" A test is given Dear ones, Dear heart, so that one can reevaluate their choices. They can then reevaluate their perspective and they can move on in their own spiritual evolution.

POLARIZATION AND DIVERSE EXPERIENCES

Have you not noticed with major events, that many feel polarized. This polarization can bring great fears for those who hold peace within their heart. But also, in that polarization, there is also a shift in perception, in perspective, allowing the soul to be able to see again from a different viewpoint. This allows a plethora of lessons to come forward for the soul in its growth and evolution. Now there are those who will say this is just duality. Duality bringing forth its many, many travails but it is also, Dear ones, Dear hearts, a place to gain experience without judgment. There are many experiences that come forward in this life on the Earth Plane and Planet; experiences of being the victim; experiences of being the oppressor; experiences of being the leader; experiences of being led; experiences of feeling passion within the heart; experiences of being led blindly; so many experiences Dear ones, Dear hearts, that come forward in these situations.

THE MASTER LEADS THROUGH UNIVERSAL LAWS

Now, as you well know, it is never up to the Ascended Master to tell you what to do. It is never up to the Master Teacher to tell a student what will happen. It is only up to the Master to guide and lead through the universal laws. This you understand Dear ones, Dear heart, that the application of the universal laws will lead you truly beyond duality...will lead you to the solace...will lead you to that effervescent drink. The Cup of Balance is always there Dear ones, Dear hearts. Neutrality always exists for those who have the eyes to see and the ears to hear.

THE CALM OF "KNOWING"

At this time, this test brings about a great search for inner peace. Inner peace is always what man is truly seeking, for in that inner peace comes the silence. It is in this Great Silence that all acceptance becomes as ONE, all experiences become as ONE. In this moment, search for the inner peace. Find the Master within, as I have stated before. There you will find that inner garden that we have traveled to so many times before. There you will be refreshed. There you will find solace. Now travel with me Dear one, Dear heart. Let us find the calm there in that center of balance, there in that center of true knowing.

Choice becomes not a quandary, but is seen as an alignment to your Divine Will. This Divine Will that flows through you, flows through all of the universe. This interconnectedness of this will is in all things, flowing and letting life produce its glory. The Divine Will works out this Divine Plan, flowing in a harmony and a rhythm. The Divine Plan and the Divine Will flow beyond duality, as you well know, Dear one, Dear heart. Beyond duality lies what you have always known as the Christ Plane. Here, in the Christ Consciousness, we urge you to bring yourselves and rest. In this Christ Consciousness is where all beauty lies, where cooperation, harmony, and true Brotherhood and Sisterhood await.

AGGREGATE BODY OF LIGHT

The prophecies that we have brought of the Earth Plane and Planet, the Prophecies of Earth Change, have all been a backdrop for you to understand the need for peace and bringing this inner peace into a collective Oneship. This Plane of Christ Consciousness is indeed Unana. Unana exists for you to partake of. It brings with it an effervescent energy, an immortality of consciousness, that aggregate body of light of ONE. Light the aggregate body of light among humanity. Light and keep this light burning throughout you, throughout the day. If you are feeling fear, if you are feeling vengeance, if you are feeling anger towards your Brother, it is important to keep the Flame of Love within your heart.

It is important to keep the Light of the Christ Consciousness burning within your rational mind. Remember Dear ones, Dear hearts, those who have the eyes to see and the ears to hear, also have the heart that is open. This open heart is the Heart of Compassion. It understands the suffering that happens in the plane of duality. It understands the pain of those who have suffered loss. It is important to understand also, that in this situation where pain and loss has happened, indeed in both sides involved, is again the Law of Attraction. Understand, it is a place that you have been brought to, to learn, to perfect, and to move in your evolution. But when one knows and applies the higher laws, one then knows to call forth that Violet Flame into its mighty activity.

VIOLET FLAME TO OPEN LIGHT

As I have stated so many times before, the Violet Flame brings the consciousness to a higher level of understanding. It transmutes any given situation into a higher understanding. At this time, it is important for all chelas to bring forth, to call forth, that mighty flame in action into any circumstance in their lives that they do not find to be in balance, do not find to be in harmony.

> Mighty Violet Flame blaze forth from
> the heart of the Central Sun.
> Leap into my heart and light the Flame of Compassion
> within me.

As you well know Dear ones, Dear hearts, when the Violet Flame is brought into its mighty activity, situations of the severest are softened. An opening of light then occurs. One then sees at the end of the dark tunnel and hope. Know in the darkest of hours that the Violet Flame has been brought to bring hope, to instigate a rational mind to move forward into activity. Questions?

VIOLET FLAME FOR OUR WORLD LEADERS

Response and question: *Yes. When a group or a nation feels sorrow and pain, a rational mind may not be easily accessible. A rational mind can elude, not only the population, but also the leaders of the world. Is there anything to help these leaders?*

Each chela can call forth from their own authority, from their own God I AM, that embraces the world within the Violet Flame:

> Mighty Violet Flame, in the name of God that I AM,
> embrace this entire planet and flood it with the light
> supreme of the Violet Ray. May the Violet Flame enfold all
> leadership of this world
> and align the harmony of the spheres through
> the Great Law I AM.
> So Be It.

Response: *So Be It.*

You see again, when this law is called into its eternal activity, all is brought again to a higher frequency, a higher vibration. Then that Law of Attraction is called in again, is it not? And only a like vibration can attract a like vibration. Do you understand?

"THE ANSWER IS NOT SIMPLISTIC"

Question: *Are you saying that what occurred at our World Trade Center and at the Pentagon are only like attracting like?*

As is in everyone's daily world, those who are learning through the dual experience, all is always seeking balance, is it not?

Response: *Yes, all is always seeking balance. It is.*

When one understands these higher laws, they begin also to understand that the answer is not simplistic, even though it would appear to be. But do not, Dear ones, Dear hearts, be trapped by illusion. Realize that you too must move forward now in your own spiritual evolution. Peace is that which you hold within. Inner peace is that which you call upon. Peace among Brothers is again, that manifestation of the Law Eternal. Now you know, as you visualize a thing, as you see it and hold it in the out-picturing, you can bring that into the outer activity. First, it is known within the inner activity; then, it is manifested into the outer; is it not?

Response: *Yes, that is the process.*

It is true, Dear ones, in all manifestation processes but there are also those beliefs that are co-creating. Very often, we have no idea where these beliefs come from. They have come through activities of shame, guilt, processes not related to true Co-creatorship. But yet, experiences become empowering teachers, do they not?

Answer: *Yes, experiences are empowering teachers.*

TAKE TIME, WAIT, OBSERVE, WATCH

From this Dear one, Dear heart, there is no mistake ever, ever, ever. As we begin to examine the universal laws eternal, we also then begin to understand their application. This is the higher knowledge of the rational mind. Sometimes it is better to stand into the Great Silence, to take your time and to wait, to observe, watch, and listen with open ears; then, you truly can see with open eyes. It is true Dear ones, Dear hearts, that there are always conspiracies that await. There are always the evil and the dark recesses that exist in all situations. But as you well know, as I have trained you so well, is a glass half full or is a glass half empty? It is up for you to see and point out where you choose to be in your own perception of reality.

Question: *So, if the glass holds universal water and whether it is seen as half-full or the half-empty is a dualistic perception, the true perception is that it is part of the universal water?*

It is true Dear one, Dear heart. Those who understand that this is only experience then are led to that greater understanding. They are here to move beyond experience and into their true Mastery of the God I AM. Now are there any further questions?

THE CHRIST WITHIN

Question: *Is there a decree for the individuals who are feeling unsettled in their own hearts and cannot find peace that may be shared?*

In this moment, I shall step down and allow Dear Sananda to bring forth instruction.

[*Sananda requests permission to come forward, it is granted, and he begins to speak.*]

Greetings beloveds. It is important at this time for those who seek the Christ within to find it through inner meditation. First, it is important to silence the mind. This may be done with several decrees, one that the individual may choose. But bring within, an inner silence. Sit in contemplation. Gently close the eyes. Focus all energy upon the heart. In that moment of the focus of energy upon the heart, feel within the connection to all of life. Feel, as this heart is connected to all of life, the radiating pulse that is in all living creatures, that is in all living consciousness. This consciousness that permeates all living things is the consciousness of the ONE, Unana. Meditate upon this pulse. Work to hear this pulse within the inner ear. In this inner hearing comes a radiation. This radiation is the growth of a new energy body. This energy source is carried with you throughout the day. Bless all that you come in contact with throughout the day. Carry the radiance of this loving Christ throughout your day. This I encourage all to do. Questions?

Question: *Yes. In this meditation and visualization, is there a symbol that we can focus upon that would universally unite us to this ONE?*

There are symbols for all cultures and each of them mean different things to different cultures. But focus upon white and gold. This will bring about a calming and a healing effect upon the consciousness. It also brings about unification of the self. So Be It.

Response: *So Be It.*

[*Sananda is now backing away and Saint Germain is coming forward.*]

WHEN YOU ARE HINDERED BY FEAR

Beloveds, Dear hearts, there of course has been much talk among the Great White Brotherhood and Sisterhood of Light, of how to approach humanity at this time. For we realize the great fear that is traveling among many. It is important to understand the work that is in front of you at this time. It is also important to understand the great God I AM that resides in each and every one of you. We have spent much time, have we not Dear one, Dear heart, speaking about the God I AM, the Master within, the Eight-sided Cell of Perfection? It is now time to reflect upon all of those teachings and bring them forward into their greater understanding. Use the meditation technique that Dear Sananda has brought forward to calm the mind.

It is also important to call upon the alchemizing, Violet Flame into all situations that you feel are being hindered by fear. Fear, you see Dear ones, Dear hearts, is a vibration that lowers frequency; that lowers energy fields; that brings about these lower animalistic qualities; that brings about a more emotional response. It is also important to stay focused upon the work at hand, to not allow the disruptions of life to come in and interrupt the greater Focus Divine. Beloved El Morya stands by my side at this moment as a reminder that the Will of God does move forward in the most mysterious of ways. Now if there are not further questions, I should like to continue.

Response: *Please continue then.*

MOVING OUT OF DARKNESS

Our work shall now continue upon dispensing information on the grid of the Earth. You see Dear ones, Dear hearts, we have spoken before of those grand intersections of lei-lines and how they do indeed create at this time a new energy or force upon the Earth Plane and Planet. It is true Dear ones, Dear hearts, that the Awakening is at hand. The time has come for man to receive the gift. Mother

Earth, Beloved Babajeran, in her own evolution, is coming forward at this time to offer herself of service. This service is bringing forward a higher frequency and a higher vibration. As you well know, the Ascended Masters have also come forward to bring their service along with Beloved Mother Earth, Babajeran.

What does this mean, when we speak of Mother Earth? Yes, we speak of her as a higher consciousness. We also speak of her as our Mother, as our Divine Mother. Yet, we also acknowledge her presence as a system, a system that we have spoken of before in our definitions of the Earth Plane and the Earth Planet. Mother Earth comes forward in her own evolution, in accordance to a Divine Plan and a Divine Will, as you well know. This science of timing is predetermined by the Ray Forces and that Great Galactic Center, or Great Central Sun, the Mighty Logos. Mother Earth, in her own evolution, has offered to sponsor those who are now coming forward to bring a higher frequency and vibration to this planet. At this time, many Ascended Beings are coming to the Earth to offer their service. But there are also the vibrations and the frequencies of new incoming souls, which have never incarnated upon the Earth before but yet, are brought here to bring a higher service. This is allowing for greater like frequencies to imbue the Earth, to bring it out of darkness and into light.

It is still possible that there will be many Earth Changes upon the Earth Plane. It is very possible that there will be changes of the Earth Planet. These changes come, shall we say, to usher in a new vibration, for like can only understand like; sameness only understands sameness; balance seeks to give balance. This is an important teaching to know and to understand; for in this time, Mother Earth will come forward, working at will, in accordance with all Ray Forces, to bring forward this higher frequency, a Golden Age, a Golden Time.

We have spoken about Kali Yuga. We have spoken of the consciousness of Dvapara Yuga. We now know and understand that it is a matter of your own personal, individualized consciousness, whether you are presently within one or the other. Yet, there is the potential and the possibility, through desire, to raise all in consciousness. This group consciousness could bring forth even a higher vibration, a higher quality. It is true Dear ones, Dear hearts, that Mother Earth at this time may go through many rumblings in this massive change but, if assisted by those who have the eyes to see and the ears to hear, this too could be a much gentler birth of consciousness. That is why we have given the instructions on the Golden City Vortices. That is why we have given instructions of the many lei-lines in their intersections, so you can bring this into a greater understanding.

THE GOLDEN CITY STAR

We have outlined and given the teachings of the Doorways of the Golden Cities, but it is important too that we understand the work and the functions of the Stars. For you see Dear ones, Dear hearts, the Stars are indeed the most powerful areas of influx in any Golden City. They work as a radiating nucleus of the original intention of the Ray Force. From there, the Ray Force enters; from there, the Ray Force permeates; from there, the Ray Force influences. That is why we have asked for those who wish to bring their own personal, individual alignment into a greater harmony, to go to the Stars to seek in solace and prayer and to find, in their own inner meditation, the contact with their own Master within. Finding their own answers, they can then work in harmony with the influence of that particular focus.

This is also why Stars of Golden City Vortices have been earmarked as places for ceremonial work, as well as spiritual understanding. In times of great turmoil, they are places to go to pray for peace. They are places to go to meditate upon peace. For you see Dear ones, Dear hearts, it could only stand to reason that these vibrations then would continue to flow throughout the grid of the Earth and create a new energy, a new focus, a new vibration.

THE SILENT MASTERS

The Golden City Vortices have been brought forward to bring a greater understanding to humanity of the process of Co-creation. In each of the Golden City Vortices, a Master Teacher stands at each of the points on the gateways. Some Master Teachers are well known. Some are silent, always guiding, but yet in their own quality of service, they come forward leading and guiding humanity into greater evolution, into greater hope, into greater light. Know that the work is unfinished but yet within you is perfection. This perfection is and always will be, but that perfection too is waiting to be released, to express its highest potential. Dear ones, Dear hearts, questions?

INDIVIDUALIZATION UPON A RAY

Question: *In these Stars are the Ray Forces that you may be attracted to, to work with for your own transformation and the transformation of the Earth Plane, is this true?*

This is true Dear one, Dear heart. Each individual, at any given moment, is a little different. For instance, one person who may have a dominance with the Green Ray is suddenly feeling the influx of the Ruby and Gold Ray; therefore, they travel to Malton to continue their work. Another who is has always felt an alignment to the Violet Ray, suddenly feels in harmony with the work of the Blue Ray and an alignment to the Divine Plan. You see, the Ray Forces and the Golden Cities indeed are Temples of great Consciousness, that have been brought forward as a grand Divine Intervention. The assistance is there Dear ones, Dear hearts. We stand in guard of these Temples. We stand in eternal protection.

SEVEN POINTS PER DOORWAY

Question: *The points that you are referring to are the points that form a Maltese Cross on the surface of our planet?*

In one Doorway, for instance, there are up to six different points total but seven is the aggregate of each of these combined. So seven points exist within each Doorway. Do you understand? [See Appendix F, *Adjutant Points of a Golden City*.]

GOLDEN CITY RETREATS

Question: *Yes. And so you are saying that there is an Ascended Being, an immortal, if you will, in each of these points?*

It is true Dear one, Dear heart and they stand guard over their own individualized retreat that exists over that point. That is why, in the Golden City Vortices, there is so much potential and possibility for spiritual growth, for spiritual evolution. As we move into this Time of greater Light, these cities will grow in greater and greater appearance. For those whose eyes are clearly opened, they will see them at times as if they were resting gently in the heavens. But it is true Dear ones, Dear hearts, even for those who yet do not see, but know the truth in their heart, they do exist. Proceed.

THE MASTER APPEARS

Question: *So, as a spiritual journey, as a personal path, any individual who feels called to take a map and go to these areas to search is being called to their own transformation?*

It is true. But know this, within the Law Eternal, there is no mistake ever, ever, ever. Dear ones of humanity know this: Let your hearts unite as ONE...follow that Law of Love supreme...and *there* is healing grace. So Be It.

Response: *So Be It.*

Questions?

Question: *So, we are to encourage those aware of the I AM America Material of prophecy to travel to these Points and Stars as they feel so guided?*

When the student is ready, the Master indeed appears.

Response: *This is true. It appears to give the student the discipline that is necessary for their growth. There is not much that I can say about that other than it is an individual choice. And it is truly in my heart that all those who will hear this or see this in print, will be called and will go and follow that calling.*

For those who have the eyes to see and the ears to hear, know that I AM.

Response: *So Be It. I have no further questions.*

9

Unified Plane of Understanding
Saint Germain

Greetings Beloved chelas in that mighty Violet Flame. I AM Saint Germain and I request permission to come forward.

Response: *Please Saint Germain, you are most welcome. Please come forward.*

DURING TIMES OF FEAR

Greetings Beloved Dear ones, Dear hearts, chelas of mine. Yes indeed, during times like this, there is much turmoil upon the Earth Plane and Planet. Many still feel great sorrow and fear but let me assure you Dear ones, Dear hearts, that peace reigns supreme. Carry always peace within your heart. Call upon that mighty Violet Flame to transmute any discord, any disharmony you may be feeling in the current situation. Always know Dear ones, Dear hearts, that we are always there, stalwart Brothers and Sisters by your side. Know that we are always there to lift you through any situation, any circumstance that leads you into great fear, that leads you into any situation where it may be hard for you to make a choice for peace.

Know Dear ones, Dear hearts, that we have traveled this path before. Know, in our embodiments upon the Earth Plane and Planet, that we too knew of these times of war upon the Earth Plane, knew of these times of great fear and experienced great fear ourselves. Know that through the transmutation process and keeping our focus upon the ever-present ONE, seeking harmony first within the heart, that we were always then able to overcome situations. Know Dear ones, that we are always there standing by your side, ready to help and give you assistance in your path leading to the Ascension and spiritual liberation.

Dear ones, Dear hearts, life is filled with many experiences…experiences of joy…experiences of life. Also know that life holds experiences of pain and experiences of death. This is duality Dear ones, Dear hearts. It is how the soul learns. It is how the soul chooses. You see at this time you are being presented with a choice. It is that simple. Do I choose fear or do I choose love? It is always that simple. Even in the Teachings of Prophecy, it always comes down to a simple choice. You know the difference between the vibrations of fear and when you experience the vibration of peace and love. It is that simple in understanding that Law of Attraction.

When you call upon that mighty Violet Flame, not only does it bring your heart to that feeling of peace, to that location mathematically of neutrality, it also charges all of your energy fields electromagnetically. And in that moment, you come to a different understanding. Through this charge within the electromagnetic field, comes forward a different attraction, does it not? All is based in duality upon that Law of Attraction. You are constantly attracting unto yourself that focus of your desire. It is true at all times, Dear ones, Dear hearts, that you are Co-creating the experience one moment at a time. Now it is important to hold that focus throughout your whole day, to constantly reassure yourself in making that choice for what you wish to create. Do I wish to create fear? Do I wish to create love? These are the simple questions sometimes presented in duality but often they are not seen.

INTENTION AND SELF EXAMINATION

Often within the travails of illusion, we see fear disguised as love, love disguised as fear. It is important always to question the self. Is this appearance only, or is there more that lies behind this? We have taught you Dear ones, Dear hearts, that in creation, intentions are very important. For you see intention also helps to determine the outcome. What is the intention here? Why am I doing this? What is the purpose of this creation I am now sending forward? Sometimes this takes a brutal honesty of the self, examining intention, examining the how and whys of the self. Sometimes the self-examination turns one so inward, they no longer relate to the outside world. But yet, the outside world is there to mirror back and show you how powerful you are Dear ones, in the use of the God I AM.

BALANCING THE DUAL FORCES

You know that you are here to gain a Mastery of the forces, to begin to understand the dual reality and how it exists. Look at your body. Contained within your body is a masculine side and a feminine side. You have left and you have right; two arms and two legs. You also have two ears and two nostrils through which you breathe. When you look at the body, you see duality mirrored throughout. There is the inner expression; there is the outer expression. In this Time of great Change, we have come forward to bring you assistance in leading you onward into understanding the uniting of these two forces within the self and how they can create a balance and a harmony within. To bring the dual forces into greater balance, call upon the mighty I AM. Call upon the Violet Flame to bring yourself into this greater harmony, into this greater balance.

> Mighty Violet Flame, come forth
> through the dual expression
> and raise all energies to the Plane of the Christ I AM.

When you call upon this force, you are uniting the energies within the body. You are bringing them to that neutral point where they come not only to a balance, but to a harmony and an expression that allows entry into the Plane of the Christ energy. The Christ energy, you see Dear ones, Dear hearts, accepts all sides as even. It accepts and judges with complete tolerance. It comes forward with complete acceptance. It allows all creation to exist, as it is in its complete perfection.

TIMELESS, BREATHLESS ENERGY

In the experience of the perception of duality, it feels like things are not balanced. It feels like things are not just, that things have not been righted and must be brought to balance. Please understand Dear ones, Dear hearts, that when one rises in consciousness to this unified plane of understanding, everything then becomes right. Everything becomes balanced. Everything is in the right place, as it should be. This contains a great power, a great power to promote harmony, and a great power to promote abundance for all peoples of the Earth. It contains within it a perpetual energy, for lack of a greater understanding, an energy that moves beyond the solar light. This energy is timeless. This energy is breathless.

"THE DIVINE PLAN IS ALWAYS WORKING"

Dear ones, moving into this energy of unified knowledge, that Plane of Unana, brings one to the gentle peace that the heart requires; brings one to this greater understanding of the I AM and the force of the I AM. It brings its healing solace to those who seek ease...to those who seek release from pain, not only of the physical, but pain that is contained within emotional fields and mental fields. It releases the power of the rational mind and then one is able to see, with clear understanding and concrete knowledge, how all works together for the greater whole. At times, it is difficult to see in duality just how things do work together but know and trust Dear one, the Divine Plan is always working. It is difficult to understand sometimes why a thing must be the way it is but know and understand this, from the perspective of the Christ Plane, all is in balance; all actions or karma are coming together for their complete purpose.

Now let us move on. Before I proceed with more information on the Golden City Vortices, are there questions?

BEYOND DEATH AND SEPARATION

Question: *Yes, those who have lost loved ones, who have lost at financial levels, who face the loss of a job, and can only sense suffering, loss, and doubt, how do these people sense that everything is right with creation or call God I AM into action and the Violet Flame to bring balance?*

What we are speaking of are levels of consciousness and the experience of perception. Let me explain. In the simplistic understanding of the Monad, of the ONE, of the one consciousness, there is no perception per se of separation. There is no perception but that one perception of life. All life exists for the purpose of life. When life is no longer, there is even no perception of death. All exists for the one plane of understanding, which is life itself. When one moves into duality, one begins to understand that there is life and death. One begins to understand that there is fear and love. But there are two sides to every coin; two sides to an argument; two sexes involved; left and right; up and down; forward and backwards. The pairs of opposites come forward in their multiple mirrors to give a greater understanding of life itself, the function and the purpose of evolution.

When moving to a different perception, a different understanding beyond duality, one then sees another plane of understanding, where perhaps all are existing simultaneously. And indeed, it is true. For from man and woman a child is born. This plane of understanding is brought together, this uniting of forces of negative and positive produces another plane that is called a plane of neutrality. From this comes the development of the will, a development known as choice. Choices can lead one back into polarization, into left or right, forward or backward, up or down. But choices can also lead one into a greater understanding through the spiritual evolution and knowledge, a perception comes that is known as the Christ.

THE CHRIST PLANE

There can indeed be a choice for benevolence. There can indeed be a choice for peace. But not all choices are left or right, up or down. Choices can all be seen from this center point that is developed in the human too as the heart. There are those who would state that the heart and the mind are at constant war within the human but there is a development of the heart and a development of the mind that leads one then into this greater union of understanding, that produces a higher quality of consciousness. This higher quality of consciousness is known as the Christ Plane. It is there, where all comes together in reconciliation, that one is able to see that *it is as it is*. Questions?

Response: *You are addressing individuals whose perception is developed to a certain level to even consider what you say. But for the masses who are suffering, these concepts are very far from their perception.*

But yet so many times, I remind you Dear chela, knowledge is not for the un-initiate.

Answer: *I would never disagree with that, but it is my desire to build a bridge to those suffering masses, to help them understand the sense of balance that does exist.*

> Mighty Violet Flame blaze in, through, and around
> this situation and circumstance.

>   Raise all vibration into the balance
>   and harmony of the Christ Plane.
>   So Be It.

Response: *Let their perception be adjusted, so that suffering will be lessened. So Be It.*

Questions?

Response: *I do have a group of questions but I would like those to be asked at your completion of the discourse. Please continue.*

USE OF MEDITATION

Now let us continue with the work at hand. In our last session, Dear Sananda came forward and gave you information regarding a meditation of the heart. Of course, all meditation is good at this time Dear ones, Dear hearts, any meditation which can lead you into the access of a new perception, a new understanding which leads you into access of this Christ Plane. It is important, in such times where there is such turmoil within duality, where the extremes are meeting with such viciousness on a daily basis, to quiet your mind and heart and lead it into this greater understanding.

As you well know, the use of the Violet Flame is always brought forward prior to meditation, for it brings a purification of the electromagnetic fields. It also brings a purification of the room in which you are bringing forth such a statement or decree. It allows a rhythmic harmony to bring forward a higher vibration, a focus of the will into the activity. As I have often stated before, when two or more are joined in the decree, a greater focus, a higher energy is achieved. When three, four, or five are added, again there is even a greater strength that is added to that focus. But it is always ideal to gather in groups of seven. For you see Dear ones, Dear hearts, then a complete resonation occurs, not only with the Chakra System, but also with the energy fields.

GROUPS OF SEVEN

You well understand how the septenary order is related to creation and Co-creation activity on the Earth Plane and Planet. When these groups gather in groups of seven and then move into a group or collective meditation, again a greater force is then acquired. As Dear Sananda taught in the last discourse, this meditation technique does indeed begin to build a larger energy field individually, but yet, this energy field is also built collectively within that group. So it is suggested that these decrees and meditations, particularly at this Time of great Testing, are used with greater efficiency in groups of seven. Also, it is important to understand that when these decrees and meditations are done in the Stars of Golden City Vortices for the focus of creating world peace and bringing more into this greater perception, knowledge, and understanding of Unana, that this creates a great and grand momentum.

Each time that a group gathers for such an intention or purpose, it is magnified by seven. That is, it is sent with a frequency and a vibration into the Earth but also into the outer layers of the field of the Earth. So you can begin to understand it, it is felt throughout the radius of the Star as high as 300 to 400 feet in vibration, just those seven gathering together. It creates a force field that is felt throughout the Star. Now remember, this force field is forty miles in diameter. Depending upon the force of the group in its decree and prayer work, it is felt for approximately three to four days afterwards. That is why decree work and meditation work that is used on a daily basis then builds a momentum that protects for years and time to come. That is why there have been monasteries and retreats that have been set up by the Great White Brotherhood and Sisterhood that are intact and in use year after year after year.

PROTECTION IN THE STARS

You must now begin to see the Stars as your new retreats, as your new monasteries; for indeed, these are the locations that have been set up and given assistance by Mother Earth and the Great White Brotherhood and Sisterhood, to build a greater protective grid about the Earth. In the Earth Changes Prophecies, you well understand the teachings that were given for the work that was to be completed in the Stars, bringing forward a protection from these types of changes. Understand Dear ones, Dear hearts, change is duality and so even in a situation where the safety of a country is threatened through acts of war and violence, that this too brings about a healing effect.

DAILY PRACTICE FOR THE GOLDEN CITY STAR

It is important to understand that the work we give to you is indeed incremental. We understand that it happens one step at a time but for those who have the eyes to see and the ears to hear, the daily calls do indeed help. It is important too, to understand that if you are not in the Star of a Golden City that, yes, you still continue with your daily decrees, with your daily meditation, for indeed this helps. But it is also important to direct, through a focus of the mind, energies towards the Stars. This can be done through simply placing the left hand over the heart and the right hand out in projection towards a visualization of the Star. I have taught you this technique in all out-picturing lessons, have I not?

Answer: *Yes you have.*

CREATING HARMONY

This is also an instruction that can be given to those groups that gather and would wish to project such energies, to begin to create this new grid for the Golden Age. You see Dear ones, Dear hearts, when things are brought into this structure and into this type of order, a different harmony then is created. Instead of ideas and thoughts brought into the dualistic qualities, one then begins to understand the importance of creating this New Time, the importance of living in the Golden Age. It is true that what a man thinks, he brings into creation to himself. Know and understand, as all thoughts are brought of peace, what then would you bring unto yourself but peace?

This mighty Law of Attraction is always working its great wonder at all times. It is true that if a man thinks of violence and death, he attracts violence and death unto himself. But if one then becomes focused upon these higher vibrations, upon the higher laws eternal, one then can create harmony, one then can create peace. It is a matter of focus. It is a matter of disciplining the will. Yes, this is true, but it is also a matter of just simply taking the time to do so Dear ones, Dear hearts. Now I shall continue on with instruction, unless of course you have questions.

Response: *Not at this time, please continue.*

SPIRITUAL PRACTICE IN THE GOLDEN CITY DOORWAYS

Each of the Doorways has their own intention, as I have given in other past discourses. We all know that Northern Doors bring about great manifestations. Southern Doors bring forward great physical regeneration and healing. Eastern Doors bring about harmony in groups and collective movements of families and one-on-one situations. And Western Doors always bring about a greater consolidation of the mind. You can use the same premise Dear ones, Dear hearts, within the Golden Cities. We have chosen of course the center points, the Stars, because all energies coalesce throughout and there is a greater disbursement of these energies. They come forward in their greater intention and understanding. But to do decree work and to come forward in meditation also upon these Doorways will also bring a greater intention and quality to your Co-creations.

If you wish to bring about global healing for the planet, move your energies into Southern Doors. If you wish to bring about a greater manifestation for the world economies, move your manifestations, your decrees, your meditations into Northern Doors. If you wish to bring harmony among Brother and Sister, between all of the nations, so there is a greater understanding of the collective humanity that we share, move these meditations, move these decrees, your work together into Eastern Doors. If you wish to bring enlightenment, knowledge that will serve the greater heart of humanity, this of course includes scientific discovery as well as greater knowledge of the unified field, move your work into the Western Doors.

MASTERS OF THE HEART

Now, I have given you, in the past discourses, the points also that you can work. In these different points and locations that I have disclosed to you Dear ones, Dear hearts, are also focuses of Master Teachers. Again, as I told you in our last discourse, there are many more Masters now that are coming, for they have heard the clarion call of your prayers. It is known and understood at this time, that humanity has the opportunity to take a great leap into a new focus for peace. Those who have tread this path before you are here, Dear ones. They offer their hearts in service. They are those Master Teachers who came forward in the earliest part of this effort, to offer their focus in the center part of each Golden City, in the Star itself, to anchor that Ray Force firmly into its action and activity.

A TEMPLATE IN PLACE

Now all five Golden Cities of the United States are in action, working that Ray Force, bringing it forward for its higher intention and purpose and Service Divine. These points now in each of the gateways, the Doorways of the Golden Cities, are now being activated, to bring forward their greater service and understanding of Unana, the ONE, the Christ Force. This will bring about a collective force in energy across the entire planet. Now it is true that there are those Golden Cities that have not yet been activated in their full service, but yet those throughout the world can travel to them and begin to feel these energies and integrate them into their being. They can still move with that greater intention where the template is in place.

ALCHEMY IN NATURE

Five is a very important number Dear ones; for you see, it is that work of Alchemy in nature that guides the energy of the five. There are four doorways and one center point. There are five Golden Cities that exist within the United States. Five is the mystic Divine Alchemy of Nature coming into its fuller manifestation. Five also represents that from the Christ Plane. We can rise into a new energy of light and sound through the understanding of the Fourth and the Fifth Dimension. Dear ones, Dear hearts, everything has moved with great timing and intention. This is the Divine Plan in its greater motion.

TEACHING AND HEALING

For those who have the eyes to see and the ears to hear, that is, they have developed the Seven Chakras and opened that Seventh Seal, are readied now to perceive at will, those Master Teachers who have come to bring their great service. There is great teaching and healing to occur among humanity. And even though it is a time where duality also plays its role, there are those who are readied who come forward now into this greater evolution. Questions?

Question: *In referring to these other Master Teachers coming forward at this particular time, you are referring to your own teachers and their teachers and so on, are you not?*

These are all members of the Great White Brotherhood and Sisterhood. For you see Dear ones, this organization moves beyond the Earth Plane and Planet. It moves beyond your own solar system. It is a group of likeness, of like vibration and consciousness. It contains within itself, yes, those teachers of the Earth, but it also contains those who understand, in a greater harmony, the working of peace. It also contains those who understand, in a greater harmony, the Great I AM. It also contains those souls who understand that freedom must be held and protected.

The Earth schoolroom is not the highest in terms of vibration and it is not the lowest. It is indeed, shall we say, a midrange frequency. Now you must understand too that like attracts unto like. And only so much can be bourn by one planet, one schoolroom at a time. The light work that has occurred during the Time of Transition is now allowing this greater frequency to come forward and greater opportunity now awaits humanity. But again, as you well know Dear one, Dear heart, it is only through choice. Questions?

THE TEMPLE DIVINE

Response and question: *Yes. Then a suggestion for the masses of humanity is to choose peace, to choose love, to choose abundance, to choose harmony, to choose alignment to the Divine Plan and the Divine Will and then it becomes so, is this not true?*

It is true. Mankind is indeed awaiting the Temple Divine. It is here but it must be realized. It must be activated. It must be put into its Divine Motion. Questions?

Question: *And that Divine Motion comes specifically through individual choice, the development of the will, is this not true?*

It is true.

Question: *And so for an action to come into reality or manifestation in the duality, the first step is choice, is it not?*

As I have often reminded chelas, choice is divine. Beloved El Morya often says choose, choose, and then choose again. For in choice, the soul then gains education, gains that experience that is ever so important. But in these teachings, one begins to understand the power of choice, the nature of choice; not blind and random choice, but they begin to understand their own God I AM, that source within that brings forward a greater Co-creation. Dear ones, Dear hearts, it is important to focus upon your self-Mastery at this time. It is important to focus upon the lessons that you have been given and bring them now into greater action. As I have often stated, when a test is in front of a student, that means that the student is ready. As you have always understood, this again is vibration; this again is the Law of Attraction. Questions?

Response and question: *Yes. And so as we all face these tests, all of us here in this plane of duality of the Earth, we are facing tests in the Divine Plan that we are prepared for and we can choose in such a manner to bring forth our great desires of harmony, abundance, prosperity, peace, love, and joy. We can bring these forward through our choices and our actions, is this absolutely so?*

So Be It.

Response: *So Be It. I have no further questions with regard to this part of the discourse but I do have some questions that have been sent in to us, if you can stay.*

Proceed, for this is the service that I offer.

CO-CREATION THROUGH OUR BELIEFS

Question: *A person asks, "It is my understanding that there are only two anointed messengers for the Great White Brotherhood, is this true?"*

An anointed messenger? Dear ones, Dear hearts, we must speak now of vibration again, for there are those who, through their belief systems, must have things in a structure and in such a manner that they can relate to it, so that they can grow through it and understand. This is no different than any other type of organized religion. This is not to say that organized religion does not have its place, does not have its meaning, does not have its particular structure that helps a person to grow and to learn. But beliefs are indeed beliefs. We move through them all the time. We choose our beliefs. Through these beliefs, we create. In these creations and also Co-creations, we come to a greater understanding of self and move forward in our own soul's evolution. There are those who have been brought forward to bring such a purpose, to bring that movement of energy forward, to bring that teaching forward. As you well know, as I have spoken to you Dear one, Dear heart, there is a particular focus and energy to this work. Very often, I do not bring you information from what others are learning and in this case, these particular anointed messengers are working for their particular focus, for their particular energy of that which they are learning in helping others.

THE MASTER LIES WITHIN

We must move beyond judgment. We must move beyond critical analysis. Is this person the one? Is that person the one? We are always waiting for the one who has the greater knowledge, the greater insight. It is important to understand that the Master lies within. That is why an Ascended Being will never tell another what to do.

We will only make a suggestion and give assistance, to bring that one into higher vibration, into higher understanding. To see the universal laws and how they are applied can help to bring one into greater understanding of the Ascension process.

TOLERANCE

This is not to say that one path is better than another; for indeed, we all have the individual will. One may not understand the individual karma that one is dealing with; one may not understand the individual's dharma or purpose that one must now bring forward. I ask that we judge not, that we allow with complete tolerance. These messages do exist. But again, it does require choice and that choice is based upon your heart. It is also based upon the vibration and energy that you have achieved at that given moment. Look back but just a few years Dear ones, Dear hearts and you will see the growth that you have made during these Great Times. Know this, in this work that I bring forward from the great heart of I AM THAT I AM. I AM Saint Germain and I blaze forth on that Violet Flame of Mercy, Transmutation, and Forgiveness. So Be It.

Question: *So Be It. It would seem to me that it would be more a matter of choice, what particular resonation or vibration of teaching a person decides to embrace, is this not so?*

If this individual is drawn to this vibration, to this energy, and is growing and learning through it, then one must never interfere with another's path. For you see, sometimes what is poison for one is bread for another. It is important to move forward and to exercise the will, to bring it into greater understanding. There is no mistake, know this Dear ones, Dear hearts, ever, ever, ever.

Response: *Thank you. I understand that.*

10

Principles of Harmony
Saint Germain

Greetings Beloved chelas in that mighty Violet Flame. I AM Saint Germain and I request permission to come forward.

Response: *Please Saint Germain, you are most welcome. Please come forward.*

Let us discuss again this sacred fire, the Violet Flame. It comes forth to bring, not only its alchemizing transcending Fire of Freedom, it also brings forth a most soothing effect, does it not Dear ones, Dear hearts? For the Violet Flame opens the Heart of Compassion and as you well know, then love streams forth from the Heart of the Mighty Logos. Dear ones, Dear hearts, there is much work for us still to impart.

ACCEPTANCE OF ALL

Today I would like to bring a discourse on harmony; for you see Dear ones, when you begin to understand the Principle of Harmony, you are then able and willing to enter into a new vibratory rate. You are then ready and willing to enter into a new state of consciousness. Harmony, as you know Dear ones, Dear hearts, is that First Jurisdiction. We have spent much time working on the Jurisdictions, but today I would like to bring forth a refresher course. Harmony sees that all sides of any issue are in complete balance. Harmony, yes, indeed streams forth in any given situation.

Harmony knows nothing of duality; there is no right and no wrong; there is no darkness; there is no light. And yet from that point of neutrality streams forth the greatest of lights, a light that is not differentiated by color but accepts all for the point of enlightenment.

BALANCE

Harmony is a foundation principle, one that the New Times will be built totally upon. Harmony of course is that founding principle that is brought forth in the Golden City Vortex of Gobean and all those who enter this Golden City Vortex begin to feel harmony and its effect upon the central nervous system. Harmony brings all within a balance. Harmony does not know or understand an element of disease, for harmony is brought to all ease. Harmony Dear ones, Dear hearts, is indeed your eternal friend, setting the way for you to see the higher way to be. It is important to understand that harmony acts within itself and unto itself, feeding unto itself in a perpetual motion, a motion of likeness. This motion is beyond the Law of Opposites, attracting unto itself more of itself. Do you see Dear ones, Dear heart, how it then brings forward an environment for pure abundance?

CALM

Harmony brings likeness unto itself always, not dividing itself, but multiplying itself. Harmony also contains a sense of peace. Harmony contains a sense of solace. Harmony Dear ones, Dear hearts, Dear friends of mine, as the First Jurisdiction, becomes a springboard for you to understand states and levels of consciousness. Harmony is always that which is felt first when the Violet Flame is invoked in its use and understanding. Harmony is a great equalizer in this sense, for harmony calms down all energy fields. In essence, any ripples, any discord, any sense of uneasiness that you may feel carried out within the energy fields, are then brought to a calming effect.

Tranquility is then sought through the Principle of Harmony and one may be brought to higher inducements and states of understanding. Energy fields are always brought into a balance with the concept of harmony. Meditating upon this one simple understanding can bring great peace to the soul.

ONENESS

Harmony, since it does not know disease, brings the energy fields to a state of Oneness. This Oneness is the great mystery that humanity seeks, for this Oneness is indeed the higher state or evolution of consciousness that all are moving towards and beginning to understand. Harmony is this first founding principle. In other times upon the Earth Plane and Planet, harmony was always the first principle used in the foundation of any governing body. It is always the first foundation to bring forward a marriage or union. It is always the principle of raising a child. It is the principle always in forming a family.

A DAILY PRACTICE FOR HARMONY

Harmony, you see Dear ones, Dear hearts, brings forward a rejoicing energy that allows for the aboundness of life, as taught in the Second Jurisdiction. For harmony knows that joy will come forward in its greater movement and greater understanding. Harmony understands that poverty has no place in its conscious field of activity. Harmony has always been a principle that Beloved El Morya has brought forward. Harmony is also a principle that Archangel Michael has brought forward in his service to humanity. Harmony comes forward, streaming from the Heart of the Mighty Logos, the Great Central Sun.

Harmony, you see Dear ones, Dear hearts, has a great foundation. It allows for true teamwork to come forward. Have you not noticed that in any great effort upon the Earth Plane and Planet, that harmony is that principle which is underlying the greater intention? When you set an intention for harmony in all things, at first you may notice that things are falling out of their regular order; things are moving in different directions; one scurrying here, one scurrying there, but each is getting in their proper position and in the right placement to bring forth balance. Balance sometimes appears to be a juggling act, but balance is always eternal, Dear ones, Dear hearts. All is moving forward with an acceptance, with a tolerance, with its greater understanding that the ONE is existing in all situations and in all circumstance. Harmony is an important principle to begin to apply into your daily life, into your daily world. Call upon the mighty I AM Presence to promote harmony in all aspects of your life.

> Beloved mighty I AM THAT I AM…
> Harmony stream forth from the Heart of the Central Sun, the Mighty Logos. Harmony, stream forth into my outer world, into all my daily activities.
> Harmony take hold. Harmony I AM.

This simple command allows harmony to come into any activity, any action. Whether it is inner peace that you are seeking or the outer manifestation of this peace that you know so securely internally, this decree calls forth through the Great I AM, that harmony within the working of yourself. Harmony, Dear ones, Dear hearts, has its greater working with all of the Ray Forces. There is not one Ray Force that knows or understands harmony any better. But for your understanding, it has always been identified more with the Blue Ray; for the Blue Ray has brought harmony into an external function for a greater understanding of it. But as you will note, all Ray Forces contain this element and aspect of harmony.

Look at the colors of the rainbow, how all colors work together. Not one is saying, "I am greater; this is lesser; I am more; this one is not the color; this one is." This is rather ludicrous, is it not, from this perception of understanding? Harmony lets all flow; lets all exist within the ONE. The rainbow spreads across the sky. It does not question which color shall be most dominant, but all come forward, do they not? They offer their brilliance and in that combination, in that great teamwork that comes forward, is the expression of harmony. That is why the rainbow is always the symbol for harmony. It is always the symbol that is used to evoke peace.

HARMONY VIBRATES AT THE HEART CHAKRA

There have been many talks now upon the Earth Plane and Planet. "How do we pursue peace? How do we begin to understand peace?" It is through the simple Principle of Harmony and there and then, all the other Jurisdictions that follow—Abundance, Clarity, Love, Service, Illumination, Cooperation, Charity, Desire, Faith, Stillness, and Creation—bring their manifestations forward. Harmony, you see Dear ones, works on a higher Principle of Cooperation. It works without judgment. It works with willingness. It works with acceptance, not just tolerance, but an acceptance that comes forth from a loving heart. Harmony vibrates at the Heart Chakra. It understands that hearts must meet as ONE and realize that all are united in one intention, in one ensuing condition. This one ensuing condition is humanity, Dear ones, Dear hearts. Yes, you all wish to move through your evolution…you all wish to move beyond the human…you all wish to serve in a greater capacity and greater Mastery. Harmony moves you together and lets you work as people, heart-to-heart, one-to-one, in this greater understanding. Questions?

Question: *Yes. Is there a progression, such as, harmony starts with a sense of tolerance, then willingness, then acceptance, then balance, then to harmony?*

There is a progression, yes, Dear ones, Dear hearts, and as they are understood and integrated within their understanding, in their activity within the experience, they are then understood as one energy.

HARMONY BUILDS A FORCE FIELD

Question: *To get to this level of harmony, is it a step-by-step movement of your conscious focus, what you're paying attention to?*

It builds an energy. Even in this moment, can you feel the resonance of energy as it vibrates, moves, and builds? For instance, now let me give you the experience. Close your eyes. Now I shall begin to build an energy force field. Do you feel the high vibration of energy?

Answer: *Yes I do.*

Do you feel as it raises through the spine?

Answer: *Yes, I do, in the whole nervous system.*

Do you feel a tingling to the outer skin?

Answer: *Yes, I can feel it everywhere.*

This is always an indicator too of energy building, energy rising within the human physiology. Now, energy with groups contains the same systemic model. How often have you heard a quotation, or in speaking to a friend, when suddenly you are overwhelmed and you have this same sensation of energy building?

Answer: *Yes that has happened in my life.*

TWO BECOME AS ONE

When this occurs, you are beginning to enter into a harmonious consensus. This is an energy that is created as the two become as ONE. This is the beginning of the creation of harmonic fields. These harmonic fields bring a certain resonance, a force, an energy that allows for the birth of power within. This power, activated by the Eight-sided Cell of Perfection, streams forward into a higher level of energy. This accesses, as we have always known, the Christ Field, the energy often known in simplistic terms as Unana. Questions?

ONE STEP AT A TIME

Question: *And so the decree that you have just given us for the I AM Presence to come forward and to bring this harmony, this is to instill in us this resonance that you have just created, is it not?*

It can be used at all levels in the creation of harmonic energy fields. Harmony, as a principle, is an energy force that is built one step at a time. As you well know, when you begin to train a young person in the field of music, it takes time for them to understand tone; it takes time for them to understand the pitch. In this same case, when you are working with those who are beginning to understand the music of harmony, it is achieved but one step at a time. Practice, practice, practice, does it not make perfect and then permanent?

Response: *As I have understood music, harmony is the blending of elements, where each element has its individual voice and yet, as you have said earlier in this discourse, not one voice is of a greater power of force than another. All are of equal value.*

Music is perhaps another great symbol to understand the energy force of harmony, where all comes together seeking a Oneship, seeking a collective expression, for lack of better language. Of course it is important, when you begin to understand these principles that take you into higher fields of consciousness and a greater understanding of your own Mastery, to apply them but one step at a time. When you are first considering these concepts, one begins to get a little overwhelmed but understand Dear ones, Dear hearts, that there are those who have tread the path before thee. There are those who come forward now and offer their assistance. Know that through the use of the Violet Flame that you can produce a calming and a healing effect upon the body.

THE BLUE FLAME OF HARMONY

Mighty Violet Flame come forth from the Heart of the Great Central Sun.
Stream in, through, and around my being.
Blaze forth the true and pure energy of the Blue Flame of Harmony.
Blaze forth within me and create a sense of supreme peace.

You see Dear ones, Dear hearts, when the Violet Flame is brought forward in this instance, it is brought to quell down misunderstandings, to bring the energy fields back into balance. Then, call forth the use of the Blue Flame of Harmony, the use of the principle itself. Now, when I speak of the Blue Flame or the Blue Ray, I give this as an illustrative fact that it brings harmony into an experiential understanding. Questions?

EXPANSION OF CONSCIOUSNESS

Response: *So in essence, the choice to create harmony is a stepping stone to expand our consciousness beyond the condition of the human consciousness into the universal.*

It is the next step of moving into the expansion of consciousness that exists for all to partake of. As we have often stated so many times, divinity is within but must be realized and understood.

THE CHAOS BEFORE BALANCE

Response: *That realization and understanding is truly a challenge for most of us, for we are greatly distracted by many things that have nothing to do with... well, maybe it does. It all works together.*

All does work together, Dear one, Dear heart. Remember when I told you that sometimes it seems as if all is in chaos, all is in disharmony, but perhaps what is being illustrated by that fact, is that all is moving into its greater alignment towards creating harmony. Have you ever noticed that at certain times, within the seasons, there is a freak storm? Often times this happens in early summer; sometimes this happens in early spring. But these freak storms come forth and one does not understand their purpose, does not understand their meaning. They seem to appear out of nowhere. Snow when it is summer? Or hot temperatures in the beginning of spring? But what is happening is Mother Earth, herself, is bringing forward a balancing effect for her own systems. In this same way, as you begin to study harmonic fields and their resonance, they too are seeking their own balance, as they exist in this higher understanding of consciousness. Now, I am not speaking of an individualized energy field. I am speaking of an energy field that exists between two that is created and the two shall become as ONE. Sometimes this balancing effect seems rather chaotic but it comes forward serving the greater plan. Do you understand?

Answer: *Yes I understand. So everything is as it should be in that balance of harmony, even though that may not be our perception.*

It is true, that perception is the grand creator in understanding the leverage of consciousness. Perception, or how you choose to see things, will always play a great role in the understanding of this concept.

Question: *Yes, I think I understand what you are saying. For example, the events of global warming, the ozone layer changing, what has happened in New York and Washington, D.C, and now in Afghanistan, these are all events to bring things to harmony, are they not?*

From that perception indeed and from them shall come a greater understanding of harmony and what harmony is; how it can be created to greater intensity; how we can see results from it. Now, there are results that come, you see, from different states of consciousness, from different understandings or perceptions. Harmony always brings forward a sense of peace and well being. There is always a sense of teamwork and greater union and understanding when harmony is in any given situation. There are always of course some situations where one does not feel comfortable. Some fall away from this and this is a normal reaction to that type of energy. But harmony contains also a peace that passes understanding, as you well know Dear one, Dear heart. When harmony comes to this greater understanding, it begins to build that foundation for abundance. Questions?

"HARMONY IS A LEVEL OF CONSCIOUS ACTIVITY"

Question: *So in essence, harmony is the alignment of the Divine Plan and the Divine Will and so when we see, for example, Americans having a sensitivity to each other, in contrast to the events of September 11th, when we see them announcing that they are ONE with each other, is this just the ebb and the flow needed to create that harmony once again?*

It is part of the creation process towards harmony. The United States, as an aggregate consciousness, is not yet at this level. Please understand this Dear one, Dear heart, that harmony must first be understood personally and then applied in a greater understanding, where two shall become as ONE. Proceed.

Question: *So when you are Mastering your own thought, feeling, and action, you are working to harmonize those?*

It is true Dear ones, Dear hearts, but harmony is a level of conscious activity. It is a level that one seeks towards. One begins to understand the harmony that exists within can be expressed in the outer activity as well. Harmony in groups is one way that this can be experienced at its outer manifestation. Of course, all those contained as individual members of this group also contain a level or personal understanding, a vibratory consciousness of harmony internalized within them, and so naturally through this Law of Attraction, they come together and express this harmony in a greater understanding. Proceed.

GROUP HARMONY

Question: *And so the decrees that you have just given can also be utilized to create group harmony?*

Group harmony is very important at this time Dear ones, Dear hearts. Group harmony, as it moves forward, will affect the world for greater planetary transformation and healing. As we see, if we have all those at levels of inner peace, but they cannot move together into group activity, we will not have the creation of a higher vibration upon the Earth. It would be impossible, would it not, for it to move forward? But use the model again, as you see called Mother Earth, Mother Nature. In her own seasons is that harmony, acquiescing one to the other. Each contains different elements and different scenery, different energies, but each knows how to work and blend, knows how to understand and work with one another in a group. It is important to understand that group harmony will move the Earth into the New Times, into a greater understanding.

Response and question: *I see. So it will require collective harmony, us coming together completely, to move to the next level of consciousness. This would require coming together with a single focus and intention for anything to be accomplished, would it not?*

And yet, they may also be so wonderfully individualized, as in the teaching that I gave to you on the Rays. But it is true, their intention is ONE, held upon harmony.

Response: *So as long as that is the intention, then it can be achieved.*

So Be It.

Response: *So Be It. I have some questions of a personal nature, if you will be so inclined to help with these.*

At your request Dear ones, Dear hearts, I am always available.

KARMA AND USE OF THE VIOLET FLAME

Response: *You have suggested that the Violet Flame will help the work of I AM America and our work (Lori's and Len's) to flow better. Could you elaborate?*

It will help to soften karmic implications between the two of you. Of course you see, all is brought together through that mighty Law of Attraction, all is seeking balance through that law eternal. There are those karmas that one may carry individually and another may carry individually, but when two become as ONE in the intention that they carry to create harmony, the working out of those things may create that balance supreme. That is, at times things feel quite chaotic. One may be suffering a karma from the past that must be brought to balance. The other may not understand this and then is brought to great levels of discord and disharmony, or a sense of discontentment. The work of the Violet Flame has always been brought forward for humanity to bring karmas of the past into balance, to allow the Lords of Karma to come forward and intervene at higher levels of understanding. Do you understand?

SERVICE AND THE RELEASE OF KARMA

Question: *Yes, there are balances that happen in this realm, the Earth Plane, and then there are balances from other realms, is that what you are referring to?*

It is important to understand that in this individual case, you have come forward in this, as an opportunity to move your soul forward in its own evolution. For you see, it is your service that you bring forward which helps to create a template for consciousness to flow into the future. For the messenger, it is also a situation where a blessing is being brought forward for this individual; for you see, each message that is brought forward from the other side helps lighten the karma of this individual as well. But it is a blessing in this respect, that each message that moves forward and is heard by those who have the eyes to see and the ears to hear, that they too move the Earth in its own evolution forward in a greater harmony, in a greater light supreme. Do you understand?

Question: *Yes, each plays the part. Are you saying that every time Lori brings through a message, that lightens the burdens of her karma, and the service that I bring forward helps to set those messages into the world?*

It is so Dear ones, Dear hearts. And as you understand too, the service that I bring forward for humanity helps to move the world further along, helps all to work in this greater system of awareness. It is important to not judge one another. It is important to not see one as right and one as wrong, that one is filled with karmic burdens and one is filled with blessings. For you see Dear ones, Dear hearts, life contains all these elements, does it not? With each step that you take into this material illusion, you understand this more and more. And thus begins the release process. This work that has been brought forward instigates the beginning of the release process. This is important, for you see Dear ones, Dear hearts, it is the beginning and the birth, as well as the death. Do you not see that they work hand-in-hand, one unto the other. As it has often been said, "When one door closes, another then opens."

But beyond such analogies, we must begin to understand what is really happening within this work. It is the birth of a new way of thinking. It is the birth of a new perception. It is a birth of a new form of consciousness. As I have said, the New Times will usher in a new way of thinking, a new way of being. This work is about the New Times, the new way to think, the new and many possibilities of being. This messenger has always held, in the highest intention, a possibility and probability for the birth of a great future. This soul's work has always been aligned to works that are oriented towards the future. And you, Dear one, Dear heart, who have stood and asked the questions also serve, for you represent the current day; you represent the present moment. The now is always important, is it not, in any situation, in any circumstance? Now I am not saying that your consciousness is that of the common denominator, for it is not. But the two of you are coming together, providing this as a service. Does this help?

SANANDA'S PEACE MEDITATION

Response and question: *Yes, it does. I understand your answer completely. The next question regards Sananda's meditation technique. We have been assisting the organization of many groups around the world and would like to know if you have any suggestions or insights regarding this effort?*

We are quite happy with the effort that has been made and we are getting assistance at the inner levels to allow this to move into a great momentum of light. It is important that groups are formed in all Stars for this meditation technique. It is also important to understand the Stars of all Golden Cities, activated or not activated, can also be utilized for this purpose. [See Appendix G, *Sananda's Peace Meditation*.]

Response and question: *I understand. Some individuals seem to have great difficulty going to Stars of Golden Cities. Would it be all right if we help them, in the organization of their meditation techniques, wherever they are?*

First, it is important to identify all Stars of Golden Cities. This work I now assign to you to complete, this work and this endeavor for the Great White Brotherhood. Do you accept?

Answer: *I accept.*

The next part will be to work with the left hand over the heart and the right hand projecting out during the meditation process. This brings forth a radiance. This brings forth an energy that is projected as a type of laser consciousness, projecting out through the center of the palm. Breath work can also be utilized to project the energy to the Stars. It is important that the energy is always projected through the Stars. Now, each group may work with a map if they wish, or hold a visualization within their mind's eye. Questions?

Question: *They may do this either by physically going to the Star location or by focusing on the Star location on a map? Will this be sufficient?*

Either way will be sufficient; however, physically within the Stars brings forth the greatest of energy movements. The use of this meditation technique on a weekly basis is very important; for again, as Sananda has stated, it begins the growth of the new collective energy body. It is as two shall become as ONE. It is that first experience in creating these higher forces of harmony. It is carried then individually but it is activated through group consciousness.

Response: *I see. It's the beginning steps of Unana.*

So Be It.

Response: *So Be It.*

11

Science of Solution
Saint Germain

Greetings Beloved chelas, in that mighty Violet Flame. I AM Saint Germain and I request permission to come forward.

Response: *Please Saint Germain, you are most welcome. Come forward.*

Greetings Beloveds, Dear hearts, chelas, and students of mine. There is much work for us still to discover, much more information that I must impart. Dear ones, Dear hearts, the work upon the Earth Plane and Planet that we bring forward streams, yes, upon that Green Ray of Healing and Ministration to humanity, but also streams forth on that mighty Violet Ray of Mercy, Compassion, and Forgiveness. This Violet Ray comes forward at this time in humanity's history to open the Heart of Compassion, but also to transmute karmas of the past, to bring the soul into greater balance, so that the mind is ready to receive the information that is about to be given.

AWAKENING AND MOVING BEYOND FEAR

Higher teaching, higher awareness comes forward to lead the soul into a new evolution. This evolution of consciousness leads the soul into beginning to understand how, like one building block after another, each state of consciousness is built upon the other. When one begins to move out of fear, one then recognizes and sees that they are no longer a victim of the past, that everything has happened for a reason, and everything fits together one step at a time. That is why I always say to you "move in small incremental steps and you will not miss one bit along the way." For it is important Dear ones, Dear hearts, that you understand each stage of consciousness as you move along in your own awakening, in your own evolution. When one moves beyond fear, one begins to recognize that they have touched the Master within. The Master within always has the courage to heal.

It is important always to touch the Master within, the mighty I AM Presence, this higher power that exists for all of humanity. It is the power that moves all into a greater awakening, into a greater understanding. Indeed, it is likened to the consciousness of Unana, but it is a power that moves freely. It is a power that is there to always give you help, to always give you refreshment. When I say refreshment, I always speak of the Cup, for this Cup represents the Cup of Balance. It is a Cup of Neutrality. It is filled with this effervescent energy of the I AM, the higher power, the Master within.

THE PERFECTED STATE OF THE I AM PRESENCE

The I AM Presence is the individualized Presence of God that exists within you. It is there for you to call upon at any time. The I AM Presence is your perfected state. It is how you are seen throughout the Eyes of God. At any time, it is the most perfect state of consciousness that you, as an individualized consciousness, can access. The I AM Presence is indeed the pathway of how you shall be set free. Accessing and utilizing the I AM Presence brings you into a greater and greater harmony with the ONE, with the consciousness of Unana. As you access the I AM Presence, it grows too in its own energy states.

As you have noticed in every teaching as I come forward, the energy begins at a slower rate and as we get to the midstream of each teaching, the energy is growing and growing in its release and transference of energy. It is the same too with the I AM Presence. As it is accessed by you through your conscious will, this activity releases more and more of the energy of the Great I AM. The I AM exists as a universal substance, exists as an Omnipotent or Omni-essence energy that is permeating all things at all times. But in the same way that the wind exists in the air that you cannot see as an unseen force, you at times cannot see but feel the Presence of the Great I AM.

The I AM Presence is your individualized experience of the I AM. The I AM Presence, as you begin to access it, more and more grows in energy. Each time you access the I AM Presence and call it into activity, it comes closer and closer to your daily experience of consciousness. It brings you into a greater level of awareness, a greater states of consciousness. There, you are able to accept with great willingness its ability to bring harmony into your life, to bring balance into situations, and lead you onward to the state of consciousness, the path of the heart known as love.

LOVE, JOY, AND THE MASTER WITHIN

Love, you see Dear ones, Dear hearts, through the I AM Presence, opens the door to Unana, a state of consciousness where many Brothers and Sisters of like mind reside. That is why, at this state of consciousness, one feels an overall connection to the All That Is, to all of life. At the state of love, one begins to hear the voice within and the Master within becomes individualized, the mighty Master that exists within you as the individualized Presence of God. Your divinity becomes alive. It is true in lower states of frequencies of consciousness, the God Presence is always present, but it is not as activated. It is not being used to its fullest potential. But again, as I say there is no mistake, ever, ever, ever and one step at a time, Dear ones.

Let us move Brother to Brother, Sister to Sister, heart to heart, in these incremental steps that allow us not to miss one thing along the way. Sometimes the student says, "Oh, but if only I could reach these higher states of consciousness, each problem of mine will then be removed." This is true to some degree Dear ones, Dear hearts, but it is important not to miss anything in the path of Mastery. For you see Dear ones, as you proceed through each state or level of consciousness, there is the little "aha," the little awakening that comes at each level or state, that brings such delight, such joy. It is this joy, as it opens the heart, that is so ever important. You see, this joy is the laughter of the soul. This joy brings true camaraderie for those who share along the path. This camaraderie is so important. Even in this moment, as I give this information to you, as we sit teacher to student, Master to chela, we too have grown along the way, along the path. We too, in our own experience, have developed this relationship of sharing, of laughing, of learning. Yes, it is true Dear ones, Dear hearts, we too share sorrows and we also share misgivings, but we also share joy and open the heart of love.

MOVING THROUGH CRISIS

It is said that crisis often is unifying, that it brings many together for a point of problem solving. It is true. Crisis comes forward to bring a unification of the self. In the Time of Testing, many will be tested at the ability that they are performing. But at the time when they are called to this test, when they are called to bring forward their understanding, they will wonder, "How can I proceed? How can I move forward?"

Know this Dear ones, Dear hearts, that a test is always given at the level for which one has achieved, for which one is fully capable of delivering a solution. Know this, as duality exists still for you in the present state of consciousness, there is no problem without its other side, the solution. It is important in the Time of Testing to focus always upon solutions, for in the solution is the answer that will move you to the next level, the next "aha," to the next burst of joy that will bring you into a greater evolution of consciousness. Questions?

SOLVING PROBLEMS THROUGH THE ONE

Question: *Yes. Problem and solution, is that not duality?*

Indeed, when they are viewed as polar opposites, when they are seen in a dual perspective, but the answer exists as well. Problem-answer-solution; problem-solution-answer; answer-problem-solution; when you see them all linked together as ONE, they work from a whole new paradigm of consciousness. This leads the consciousness into functioning from dual perspectives, knowing and understanding that the solution always exists, that the answer always exists, and that the problem and answer-solution function together as one greater collective. This greater collective is the Christ Consciousness. It is a state of perfection known as Unana. Whenever there is a problem, immediately you know there is a solution. Proceed.

Question: *The question then is how does one perceive the answer or the solution, when all that can be seen is the problem?*

It is important to understand that all is a state or level of consciousness. At times, there are those who are blocked only within problems. All they see are problems. It is important when this happens, to move in the juxtaposition. Again, it is perspective. Is that glass half full? Is that glass half empty? How can I make lemonade from a lemon? How can I move forward in this, one step at a time? Of course, the immediate solution is to move from a negative position into a positive position. But let us take this even one step forward. In that positive position is the solution, is the answer. They exist simultaneously as answer-solution, solution-answer; these two exist side by side in the positive aspect. The problem exists through the negative aspect. This juxtaposition of perspective, within positive levels of consciousness, creates an even higher understanding, which brings the consciousness into again a new juxtaposition.

POLARITY BIRTHS NEUTRALITY

Energy flows where attention goes, as I have always told you Dear ones, Dear hearts. But one does not understand this until they have that clear experience. When attention is placed always upon problem, problem, problem, problem, one stays blocked within this perception. It is as if they are always facing a northerly wind, blowing directly upon them, but they have not yet learned how to turn their back to the wind, so that the wind will no longer force them into one position. It is that simple, of turning around, first from negative to positive. Then, from positive, one begins to understand this plane of neutrality, where one may enter into even higher states of consciousness, where one can see through juxtaposition that all is encompassing as ONE.

To even visualize, to even ask the question, brings it into the mind that there is a problem. To have conscious recognition that there is a problem in the state of duality would immediately force the consciousness to understand and know that there is indeed an answer; there is indeed a solution. These are the dual forces at work. But beyond that is the Christ energy. The three are always married as ONE. Proceed.

REMOVING PROBLEMATIC BLOCKS WITH THE VIOLET FLAME

Question: *So, are you saying that when the problem is perceived, that moving from this negative to the positive, of knowing there is a solution, all the possibilities to solve the problem will come?*

It is true. It is the marriage of negative and positive, coming together to create yet another field of conscious awareness. When a problem is perceived, know this, the answer indeed exists. The solution then leads one into higher states of awareness and consciousness. But if one is always focused upon problems, one cannot clearly see answers. If one cannot see an answer, how could one see a solution?

Perhaps the work of the Violet Flame is one of the best, to begin to remove these types of blocks.

> Mighty Violet Flame, blaze within this problem.
> *(You can then address the problem directly.)*
> Remove all discords. Remove all disharmonies
> and allow me to see the solution to
> this problem immediately.

When you call this forward, it activates your own individualized Presence of God. You then begin to see through that new juxtaposition. You then begin to see through a new conscious awareness that there is an answer. Once the answer is given, this leads the consciousness naturally to the next level of solution. From this position, energy is then placed within the solution. From solution comes again many choices. The will then moves in greater development. The will moves forward in greater understanding. But it is as simple as growing that energy.

PROBLEMS, CHOICE, AND SOLUTIONS

Have you not noticed, there are those sad-sack human beings who are always placing energy upon problems, problems, problems, problems? They grow and escalate an energy force. They seem to walk with a cloud of grim energy surrounding them at all times. It is because their focus has been built upon the creation of one problem after another. Then, there are those who understand that a problem is merely a means to find an answer and from that answer comes even a greater opportunity, the solution. Or, shall I say, solutions, for often there are many solutions, many ways of seeing how a problem can be solved. From this comes the creative process. The will then is placed into a greater exercise, choice.

EMPOWERMENT THROUGH GOD I AM

Then one begins to see how the great God I AM and choice move one forward into understanding and applying their own will in any given situation. This allows the soul to move forward, to move into greater understandings and levels of consciousness. It is a state and a level called empowerment, where one is in touch with the Great I AM. This energy then grows with greater depths, with greater clarity. A harmonizing effect begins to take hold over the individual. This harmony then creates an energy force which becomes the growth and the fostering of positive thoughts, positive thinking. These types of individuals, when you encounter them, are as if a breath of fresh air has blown right in the door. You can note it in their voice, in their demeanor, in their posture, for they carry within them an infectious optimism. It is important Dear ones, Dear hearts, to understand this process, to call upon the mighty I AM Presence, to activate the Master within. Questions?

PROPHECY AND POSITIVE ENERGY

Question: *Yes. So for every possible scenario, prophecy, or event in an individual's life, or on the world stage, are you saying that there is always a solution, or groups of solutions?*

Prophecy is one of the greatest spiritual teachings, showing how positive energy can change the most negative of all situations. Prophecy, as you well know, Dear ones, Dear hearts, speaks to the heart of humanity, to bring about a shift in perception, a shift in consciousness. It is true, that at any time, the most negative situation can change through the work of the Violet Flame, through working with perception and consciousness, as a shift in attitude and perception. This can change the most trying of all circumstance and event. Questions?

Response and question: *So, it is truly our point of perception. We can perceive the problems, but without that balance, everything comes to a halt. Consciousness does not move on because it is that creative interaction that stretches the consciousness beyond the boundaries of its perception, is it not?*

AWAKENING THE DIVINITY WITHIN

It is true Dear ones, Dear hearts. But it is important also to exercise the consciousness. It is nothing to be taken lightly. That is why we have encouraged all students and chelas to engage in meditation at least for ten to fifteen minutes per day when they are beginning. For you see, this too builds an energy field, an energy force. It allows contact with the true self, with the Master within. The student or chela gains that contact and begins to trust that within this process, the solution always is within them. Sometimes students, chelas, when encountering a problem, perceive that the answer is out there; that the answer awaits in another individual; that the answer to all problems, to all their discomfort, lies in something that is outside of them. But know this Dear one, Dear heart, all solutions, all answers, lie within. They are contained within you as states of consciousness, points of perception, readied and willing to reveal themselves to you. This is the awakening of divinity within. It comes through the openness and the receptivity, the trust and acceptance, that the Master is truly within.

You see Dear ones, Dear hearts, it does indeed take work to reveal this Master. There is no quick fix. There is no artificial means to find this Master. You must do this work yourself. That is why meditation becomes of increasing import for those who wish to proceed to these levels of consciousness. The Heart of Love awaits you at all times Dear ones, Dear hearts. Silence yourself and receive. Questions?

EFFECT OF HIGHER CONSCIOUSNESS

Response and question: *Yes. When one actually finds solutions and has stepped onto that path of self- empowerment, would this not help many others to catch that wave of solving problems from within and help the world to move on in a collective?*

It is true Dear one, Dear heart. As I have said, "infectious optimism," for it is important to understand that as a chela or student moves and experiences within the higher states of consciousness, that they have a great affect on those who may be at lower states of consciousness. They become a magnet that draws this lower consciousness into a higher energy field. You well know, that when you bring disease into a higher vibration, it comes to a point of healing. But healing is a choice, as you well know. As one, who is filled with this higher state of consciousness, begins to help and assist many around them, these too are brought to a place where the will is brought into greater development. So you see, in the same way that I come forward this day and give my assistance, you move forward throughout your day and give your assistance and on and on and on. From this level of perception, we are all connected as ONE. This is indeed the state of Unana, although there will be those who do not perceive or understand this state. But yet again, as I have said before, that wind does exist; you cannot see it, but yet you feel it. It is so. Proceed.

Question: *With your permission, may I now go to questions that have been posed to us?*

I am always here for service. I AM Saint Germain.

TWELVE, A SACRED NUMBER OF EXPANSION

Question: *A person asks, "Is it not a fact that there are twelve planets in our solar system, thirteen including our sun. Is the hidden planet one of these planets?"*

It is true. We have spoken of this before. This paradigm of twelve, you will see throughout many schoolroom situations. For you see, it is divided equally, six plus six; six to one negative side, six to one positive side. And yet, from other points of perception, it is seen as three multiplied by four, or four by three. The potential to move from the Third Dimension to the Fourth Dimension also exists within this paradigm. But it is true that there are twelve, in the same way that there are always twelve adepts or avatars that exist at any one time on each of these twelve planets. Each exists in their own frequency, as you would understand dimensional activity. Questions?

Question: *Yes. And so that brings us to the number twelve. Is this number considered a sacred number of creation?*

For a schoolroom activity, that is why Twelve Jurisdictions have been given, for they are Laws of Jurisprudence. Based upon levels of consciousness, each one of them achieve their own level, purpose, and intention for the new creation, the Golden Age, the New Times. It is based upon an expansion of consciousness. For you see Dear ones, when one moves to another field of experience, beyond the schoolroom, one's consciousness then reaches new experiences, moving into systems that exist beyond this. However, very often they make the choice to return and to help, to give, and to be of service. This is so.

Question: *It has been thought that the planet Pluto is not really a planet, but possibly an asteroid or a moon. What is it?*

It is an ancient moon that was thrown off from a completely different solar system. However, it is now a planet that is part of this system. In the future, another planet will be identified and Pluto will, at that time, through this process of higher consciousness and greater light to the system, be identified more as this ancient moon.

Question: *I see, but for the time being in our system, it does function as one of the twelve planets?*

At this time, indeed it does. But as you see, as light from the Great Central Sun emanates more and more, bringing consciousness to a higher peak, so to speak, this light of consciousness then allows for greater discovery, for greater embracing of ideas, thoughts, and consciousness. Do you understand?

THE TWO SUNS

Question: *Yes, I do. In this continuous expansion, as more light comes from our Central Sun, does this mean that the secondary solar sun for our solar system will also be illuminated at some point?*

At the time that the two suns begin to illuminate, it is true there will be greater and greater light. At that time, as you well suspect, then twelve more planets will be added to the system. But that will not be for many more years to come.

RELEASE OF NEGATIVE TURMOIL

Response and question: *I see. That is very interesting. The energies on our planet have been fluctuating, not necessarily stable. Is there something that we are to expect in the not too distant future that would be along* the lines of a change in the Earth's grid or a tectonic plate movement? It almost feels as though there is a buildup for a shift.

There is a great buildup at this present moment upon the Earth Plane, of emotional energy that is building at a low vibration. This is the low vibration of anger, hate, and violence. It is important to continue with the Sunday Peace Meditation. This was instigated, not only to bring peace among humanity, but also to instigate a calming effect to the Earth Planet. For you see, as this buildup of emotional energy proceeds, there could be great and violent storms, which will bring adjustments then to the energetic lei-lines of Mother Earth. You see Dear ones, Dear hearts, even though humanity very often views itself as a very separate entity to Mother Earth, all are interconnected in one great system.

In the same way that I have introduced to you this principle of negative plus positive equals neutrality, the same is true with humanity and Mother Earth. When I speak of the Earth Plane and the Earth Planet, I am always addressing this as one system. The recent events among humanity, among the governments of the world, are bringing about a great emotional turmoil. This tumultuous energy must be balanced upon Mother Earth. That is why it is important to use, as I have taught you specifically and directly, the mudra which will direct energy to the Stars of the Golden Cities. This is very important.

GOLDEN CITY STAR MUDRA

Response: *I see. So, it is important that in our Sunday meditation for global peace, that we use an I AM AMERICA map or a world FREEDOM STAR map and with our left hand over our heart, we open our right hand toward the Star of a Golden City that is close to us.*

Let me demonstrate for you. In this moment, you now see how this energy is being directed from the center of my palm. It is as if a laser focus is now directing. Now direct it through the breath, drawing up from the lower chakras and projecting the energy from the heart. Do you see? Do you feel this energy source?

Question: *Yes. This now connects you with the planet, doesn't it?*

Indeed it does. And it brings forth a balancing effect that is very important at this time. For you see Dear ones, Dear hearts, as I have given and directed this to you, you will give and direct this to many others. We are all connected as ONE in this great energetic movement. Do you understand?

Answer: *Yes I do. To reiterate, so that it is clear for everyone, when we meditate, we breathe up through the bottom chakras, connecting to the Earth core, and bring this energy into our heart. We then focus it through our right hand into the Golden City hologram that is on the maps. That will enhance the actions of peace in our world.*

It is true. It brings about an energetic adjustment, directed at the lei-lines of Mother Earth. At this present moment, there are great solar storms that are beginning to erupt upon your sun. With the electromagnetic fields as they are upon the Earth, a great attraction of these storms could then also cause many severe problems upon the Earth. This brings about another energetic adjustment of Earth's energy fields. You are well aware of this, for you see Dear ones, Dear hearts, the Golden City Vortices function very much like chakras do upon the human body. In this way, humanity serves as a greater part of the system of Earth and serves to bring about a healing effect, not only for peace in the collective mind, but peace in the collective system. Proceed.

Response: *I see. So, the individual and collective focus of groups doing this meditation sets forth this new paradigm for world peace. And this expansion, or a wave of consciousness, then will take hold with all.*

For all is based upon that mighty Law of Attraction. Again, it is as simple as problem to answer to solution.

Response: *Yes, I see this. This is a very interesting way to perceive things. All problems have answers and solutions. It is the way things are structured here. I understand that very clearly now. I have no further questions at this point with regard to this specific topic.*

Then I shall take my leave from you and come forward at the appointed hour. I AM Saint Germain.

Response: *Thank you.*

Appendix A

The Three Standards: The Use of the Violet Flame, Tube of White Light, and the Protection of Archangel Michael

1. Call forth the Violet Consuming Fire: "In that Mighty Christ I AM, I call forth Saint Germain's Violet Transmuting Flame of mercy, transmutation, and forgiveness. Alchemize my lower energy bodies into the perfection of the Christ! Almighty I AM! (3x)" Then proceed with any Violet Flame decree. (Use seven times.) Suggestions are: "Violet Flame I AM, God I AM Violet Flame," or "I AM a Being of Violet Fire, I AM the Purity God desires!"
2. Call upon the Tube of Light: "Beloved Mighty I AM Presence, surround me now with the Tube of White Light, ever-sustained, ever-maintained, throughout this day and onward into night! Almighty I AM! (3x)"
3. Invoke Archangel Michael's Blue Flame: "Beloved Archangel Michael, surround me now with the Blue Flame of Protection! Protect my Violet Flame in its action and activity, protect my Mighty Tube of Light, giving me multiple layers of protection! Almighty I AM! (3x)"

Complete this spiritual practice with thanks and gratitude: "I love you, I love you, I love you! I bless you, I bless you, I bless you! And I thank you, I thank you, I thank you! Almighty I AM! (3x)

Close with Almighty I AM that I AM (9x) and OM HUE (9x). (This properly seals the decree and affirmation.)

It is suggested that for those who have not completely eliminated animal products from their diets to use the above sequence. For chelas and students who have eliminated animal products and adhere to a vegan diet, the sequence is as follows: first, use of the Tube of White Light; second, call upon Saint Germain's transmuting Violet Flame; third, invoke Archangel Michael's Blue Flame. Since this is a practice associated with purification and spiritual hygiene, the difference for carnivores and vegetarians is the cleansing through the Sacred Fire. Using the Sacred Fire removes the fear substance ingested through animal products from the physical body and light bodies, transmutes karmas, and prepares the auric field for the Tube of White Light. When the Three Standards is used by vegans, it is claimed the result of the Sacred Fire is intensified, as the Violet Flame can focus its entire energy upon the transmutation of karmas.

Appendix B

Candle Meditation:

The Candle Meditation by El Morya is one of the first steps to experience the Divine Light within and calm the mind. Use a long tapered candle, not a jarred glass candle. For this exercise a white candle is preferred, but any color should work. Light the candle and establish a constant, stable flame.

First, sit comfortably; you may use a chair for back support if needed. Look and concentrate on the candle and give attention to the different layers of the light of the flame. You will notice these layers: the outer glow; the yellow-white layer of fire; the center of the wick; and the central inner glow, which sometimes contains a blue or violet hue at the base of the flame. Focus on the overall glow of the candle until you identify the layers of light. Breathe evenly and gently as you concentrate on the light.

As you observe the Flame of Light, continue your rhythmic breath as the light begins to expand and absorb the space between you and the flame. Continue this breathing until you have established a large ovoid of light, including the candle and yourself.

Remain focused in the circle of light and you will begin to notice you are in the flame; the light is even, and it flows with your breath. You may notice a pulse in the energy field you share with the flame. At this state you are ONE with the light.

Individuals who practice the Candle Meditation have reported feeling calm and peace, even in extremely stressful conditions. Sometimes this is accompanied by a high-pitch ring. El Morya asserts the application of the Candle Meditation imparts experience with the consciousness of the ONE and develops human consciousness into the HU-man. The Candle Meditation can be performed individually or in groups.

Appendix C

Write and Burn Technique:
The Write and Burn Technique helps students and chelas transmute any and all unwanted situations and circumstances, primarily undesirable dysfunctional life patterns. A venerated practice of the Ascended Masters, this type of journaling involves a handwritten letter—a petition—to the I AM Presence for Healing and Divine Intervention. The process encompasses two objectives: identifying and releasing unwanted and outdated energy or attracting and manifesting new and evolving energies. After the letter is written, it is then burned, either by fire or by light. Most students prefer to burn by fire. If, however, you choose to burn by light, place the document under a light source for twenty-four continuous hours. Insidious problems and complex-manifestation petitions may require up to one week of light exposure. The success of the light method and the subsequent acceptance of a petition depend on the reliability of the light source; the concentration of light must be continuous and without problems, e.g. blackouts, burnouts, and so on. If the issues are profound, you may need to probe deeper by identifying and addressing personal problem or life patterns. You may also want to consider rephrasing your approach to the problem, rewriting the letter, or both. Write and burn templates are provided below.

Transmute and Release Energy Patterns: Make one handwritten copy of this letter. In the name of I AM THAT I AM, I release this to the Universe to be transmuted. (List the energy or behavior patterns you have identified. Some students also insert various alchemic decrees to the Violet Flame to dissolve, consume, and transform the energy.) Sign and date the letter. Burn the letter by fire or by light.

Attract and Manifest New Energy Patterns: Make two handwritten copies of this letter. In the name of I AM THAT I AM, I release this to the Universe to be fulfilled, maintained, and sustained in perfect alignment to the Divine Will. (List the new energy or behavior pattern you would like to Co-create.) Sign and date the letter. Burn one copy by fire or by light. Keep the other copy in a sacred place (e.g. personal altar, family Bible, favorite spiritual book) until you have achieved your goal or desired behavior change, and then burn that copy by fire.

Appendix D

The Great Purification:

Primarily considered a Native American term, the Great Purification signals the end of one period of time for humanity and the beginning of a New Time. The Hopi Prophecies state the Great Purification will occur in several stages with prophesied Earth Changes, global wars, Climate Change, and nuclear devastation by the dropping of a "gourd full of ashes."[1] The final stage, known as the Great Day of Purification, is a culmination of world and social events; the crisis will force rich and poor, "to struggle as equals in order to survive." The Hopi further prophesy that "man still may lessen the violence by correcting his treatment of nature and fellow man."[2]

The Native American Sioux tradition defines the Great Purification as an escalation of prophetic events to a point of no return. Brave Buffalo, Brule Sioux Nation states, "It is time for the Great Purification. We are at a point of no return. The two-legged are about to bring destruction to life on Earth. It's happened before, and it's about to happen again. The Sacred Hoop shows how all things go in a circle. The old becomes new; the new becomes old. Everything repeats." [3]

Contemporary prophets view the Great Purification as a time for humanity to heal and transform individually and collectively. These actions create an opportunity for the Brotherhood of Man and a new society built on the ideals of cooperation rather than competition. This viewpoint asks humanity to throw away progressive Darwinian ideals regarding modern culture and cultivate spiritual growth for humanity's survival and to heal our compromised and fragile environments. The common linear theory of time that implies that the constant drive of evolutionary progress is always bigger and better is only illusion, and perilously leads humanity to the edge of destruction. According to Prashant Trivedi, we must remember the cycles of time taught by ancient civilizations and that "Humanity was faced with the same situation about 12,000 years ago, when great floods destroyed flourishing civilizations which had become overly materialistic as they too approached the end of their age."[4]

The Great Purification signals everyone that there is the opportunity to spiritually grow and develop relationships beyond greed, consumption, and exploitation. At this critical time, our inherent Divinity can move us toward balance, away from the precipice of cataclysm. "It is up to each of us to discover the true meaning of life by inquiring within our own minds. If someone tells you how you should live, what you should do, what your path might be, and if you follow that road, it will lead you nowhere," and Trivedi reminds us that spiritual wakefulness is perhaps our greatest ally at this tumultuous time. "Learning along our path is a continuous and effortless process, but one must stay awake, mentally, and not allow oneself to be influenced by the conditioning of this world. One can only stay awake mentally with a mind that is not already conditioned by society, rules, orthodoxy, nationality, religion, and so on."[5] It is time to move away from "dying systems," and move toward self-reliance and sustainable methods that harmonize with nature and Earth.[6]

---

[1] Thomas Mails, *The Hopi Survival Kit,* (Penguin Group, 1997, New York, NY), page 209.
[2] Ibid., page 210.
[3] Brave Buffalo, "Brule Sioux Nation," http://www.dreamscape.com/morgana/hyperio2.htm, (2009).
[4] Prashant Trivedi, "The Great Purification: Creation and Destruction," http://www.osfa.org.uk/essay-32.htm, (2009).
[5] Ibid.
[6] Ibid.

Appendix E

Chakras and the Five United States Golden Cities:

GOLDEN CITY	CHAKRA
Gobean	Will Chakras Throat Chakra Third Eye Chakra
Malton	Third Eye Chakra (Pineal Gland) Root Chakra (Base)
Wahanee	Heart Chakra Throat Chakra
Shalahah	Solar Plexus Chakra Crown Chakra Throat Chakra
Klehma	Sexual Chakra (Creative) Crown Chakra

Appendix F

The Seven Adjutant Points of a Golden City Doorway:

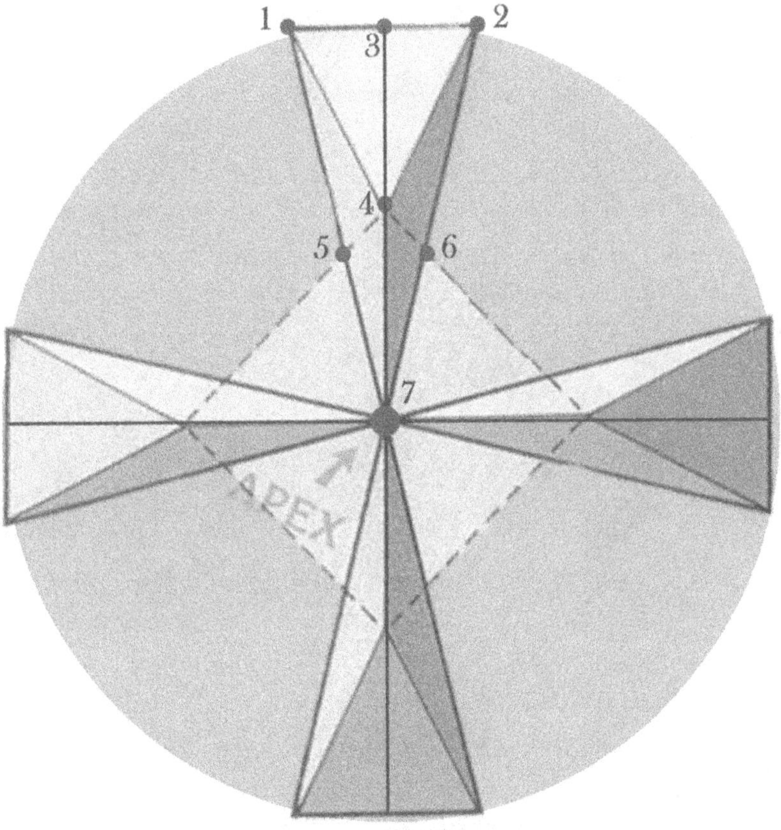

Appendix G

Sunday Peace Meditation:

In this turbulent Time of Change, Lord Sananda suggests a weekly Sunday Peace Meditation. He instructs:

> "It is important at this time for those who seek the Christ within to find it through inner meditation. First, it is important to silence the mind. This may be done with several decrees, one that the individual may choose. But bring within, an inner silence. Sit in contemplation. Gently close the eyes. Focus all energy upon the heart. In that moment of the focus of energy upon the heart, feel within the connection to all of life. Feel, as this heart is connected to all of life, the radiating pulse that is in all living creatures, that is in all living consciousness. This consciousness that permeates all living things is the consciousness of the ONE, Unana. Meditate upon this pulse. Work to hear this pulse within the inner ear. In this inner hearing comes a radiation. This radiation is the growth of a new energy body. This energy source is carried with you throughout the day. Bless all that you come in contact with throughout the day. Carry the radiance of this loving Christ throughout your day. This I encourage all to do."

Unana, or Unity Consciousness, is another name for the unified field of human consciousness. Major General Kulwant Singh of India explains, "This field of consciousness–termed the unified field in the language of quantum physics–is millions of times more fundamental and powerful than nuclear force." Major Singh, a 35-year career army veteran who helped to assemble thousands of meditation experts for peaceful defense explains, "This will produce an indomitable influence of peace and coherence in the country. No nation will ever be moved to attack India, as it becomes a lighthouse of peace and coherence to its neighbors and the world."

The Stars of Golden City Vortices function with a unique similarity to a technique developed by the late Dr. David Hawkins whose research mapped states of human consciousness known as critical point analysis. In his book "Power Versus Force," Hawkins explains his process, "Critical point analysis is a technique derived from the fact that in any highly complex system there is a specific critical point at which the smallest input will result in the greatest change. The great gears of a windmill can be halted by lightly touching the right escape mechanism; it is possible to paralyze a giant locomotive if you know exactly where to put your finger."

All spiritual practice, especially prayer and meditation is extremely effective while located in any Star area of a Golden City Vortex for World Peace. The Ascended Masters' instruction focuses on Lord Sananda's Heart Meditation and recommends that a group of seven individuals focused on this meditation can effect personal change for global peace. In essence, this technique is a force field of light, especially when applied within the Star of a Golden City Vortex, where the least amount of energy exerts the greatest effect.

A partial list of towns and cities located in the United States Golden City Stars follows. [Editor's Note: For more information see *I AM America Atlas* and *I AM America United States Golden City Map*.]

Golden City Star of Gobean
Pinetop, AZ
Lakeside, AZ
Springerville, AZ
Eagar, AZ

Golden City Star of Malton
Mattoon, IL
Charleston, IL
Shelbyville, IL
Sullivan, IL
Humboldt, IL

Golden City Star of Wahanee
Augusta, GA
Grovetown, GA
Appling, GA
Harlem, GA
Gracewood, GA
Thompson, GA
Modeo, GA
North Augusta, SC
Trenton, SC
Eureka, SC
Parksville, SC
Kitchings Mill, SC
Williston, SC

Golden City Star of Shalahah
Lolo Pass, MT
Lolo, MT
Missoula, MT
Stevensville, MT

Golden City Star of Klehma
Cope, CO

Spiritual Lineage of the Violet Flame

The teachings of the Violet Flame, as taught in the work of I AM America, come through the Goddess of Compassion and Mercy Kuan Yin. She holds the feminine aspects of the flame, which are Compassion, Mercy, Forgiveness, and Peace. Her work with the Violet Flame is well documented in the history of Ascended Master teachings, and it is said that the altar of the etheric Temple of Mercy holds the flame in a Lotus Cup. She became Saint Germain's teacher of the Sacred Fire in the inner realms, and he carried the masculine aspect of the flame into human activity through Purification, Alchemy, and Transmutation. One of the best means to attract the beneficent activities of the Violet Flame is through the use of decrees and invocation. However, you can meditate on the flame, visualize the flame, and receive its transmuting energies like "the light of a thousand Suns," radiant and vibrant as the first day that the Elohim Arcturus and Diana drew it forth from our solar Sun at the creation of the Earth. Whatever form, each time you use the Violet Flame, these two Master Teachers hold you in the loving arms of its action and power.

The following is an invocation for the Violet Flame to be used at sunrise or sunset. It is utilized while experiencing the visible change of night to day, and day to night. In fact, if you observe the horizon at these times, you will witness light transitioning from pinks to blues, and then a subtle violet strip adorning the sky. We have used this invocation for years in varying scenes and circumstances, overlooking lakes, rivers, mountaintops, deserts, and prairies; in huddled traffic and busy streets; with groups of students or sitting with a friend; but more commonly alone in our home or office, with a glint of soft light streaming from a window. The result is always the same: a calm, centering force of stillness. We call it *the Space*.

Invocation of the Violet Flame for Sunrise and Sunset
I invoke the Violet Flame to come forth in the name of I AM that I AM,
To the Creative Force of all the realms of all the Universes, the Alpha, the Omega, the Beginning, and the End,
To the Great Cosmic Beings and Torch Bearers of all the realms of all the Universes,
And the Brotherhoods and Sisterhoods of Breath, Sound, and Light, who honor this Violet Flame that comes forth from the Ray of Divine Love—the Pink Ray, and the Ray of Divine Will—the Blue Ray of all Eternal Truths.

I invoke the Violet Flame to come forth in the name of I AM that I AM!
Mighty Violet Flame, stream forth from the Heart of the Central Logos, the Mighty Great Central Sun! Stream in, through, and around me.

(Then insert other prayers and/or decrees for the Violet Flame.)

Glossary

Abundance: The second of the Twelve Jurisdictions is the principle of overflowing fullness in all situations and circumstances based on the Law of Choice.

Adjutant Point: Power points that form where the lei-lines of the geometric Maltese cross formation of a Golden City traverse or intersect. Adjutant points support the infrastructure of a Golden City, both geometrically and spiritually, and assist and disburse the unique energies held by Babajeran, the Ascended Masters, and the Golden City's Ray Force.

Akashic Record: Timeless, immortal records of all created things, especially souls and their many lifetimes.

Alchemy: The process of transmutation.

Alignment: Convergence or adjustment.

Archangels (the Seven): The seven principal angels of creation are: Michael, the Blue Ray; Jophiel, the Yellow Ray; Chamuel, the Pink Ray; Gabriel, the White Ray; Raphael, the Green Ray; Uriel, the Ruby Ray; and Zadkiel, the Violet Ray.

Ascended Masters: Once an ordinary human, an Ascended Master has undergone a spiritual transformation over many lifetimes. He or she has Mastered the lower planes—mental, emotional, and physical—to unite with his or her God-Self or I AM Presence. An Ascended Master is freed from the Wheel of Karma. He or she moves forward in spiritual evolution beyond this planet; however, an Ascended Master remains attentive to the spiritual well-being of humanity, inspiring and serving the Earth's spiritual growth and evolution.

Ascension: A process of Mastering thoughts, feelings, and actions that balance positive and negative karmas. It allows entry to a higher state of consciousness and frees a person from the need to reincarnate on the lower Earthly planes or lokas of experience. Ascension is the process of spiritual liberation, also known as moksha.

Ascension Process: The Ascension Process, according to Saint Germain, gathers the energies of the individual chakras and expands their energy through the heart. The Law of Love calibrates the energy fields (aura) to Zero Point—a physical and philosophical viewpoint of neutrality. From there, the subtle and fine tuning of the light bodies is effectuated through the higher chakras, sequentially including the Throat Chakra, the Third Eye Chakra, and finally the Crown Chakra. Zero Point is crucial in this process and it is here that the energies of all past lives are brought to psychological and physical (karmic) balance. Then the initiate is able to withdraw their light bodies from the physical plane into the Astral Light of the Fourth Dimension. The Ascension Process may take several lifetimes to complete and the beginning stages are defined through the arduous process of obtaining self-knowledge, the acceptance of the conscious immortality of the soul, and the use of Alchemy through the Violet Flame. Intermediate stages may manifest the anomalies of Dimensional Acceleration, Vibrational Shifting, Cellular Awakening and Acceleration, and contact with the Fourth Dimension. Use of the Gold Ray at this level accelerates the liberation process and unites the individual with soul mates and their beloved Twin Ray. Later stages of Ascension include the transfiguration of light bodies and Fifth Dimensional contact through the super-senses as the magnificent Seamless Garment manifests its light. It is claimed that the Golden Cities assist the Ascension Process at every stage of development. According to the Master Teachers diet and fasting will also aid the Ascension Process at various phases.

Ascension Valley: According to the I AM America Prophecies, Ascended Masters appear in physical form in the Golden City Vortices during and after the twenty-year period. At that time, Mass Ascensions occur in the Golden Cities, at the Star or center locations of these Vortices, and in select locations around the world, which are hosted by the complementary energies of Mother Earth. A model of this type of location is Ascension Valley located in the Shalahah Vortex.

At-One-Ment: The spiritual practice and state of Unity. This spiritual ideal is philosophically affirmed through the recognition of humanity's innate divinity, equality, and human connection to ONE source of creation. This results in the At-ONE-ment, and the advanced practitioner morphs into a Step-down Transformer of the Seven Rays of Light and Sound as an expression of beauty and creation. The At-ONE-ment facilitates the consciousness of Unana.

Astral Body or Plane: The subtle light body that contains our feelings, desires, and emotions. It exists as an intermediate light body between the physical body and the Causal Body (Mental Body). According to the Master Teachers, we enter the Astral Plane through our Astral Body when we sleep, and many dreams and visions are experiences in this Plane of vibrant color and sensation. Through spiritual development, the Astral Body strengthens, and the luminosity of its light is often detected in the physical plane. Spiritual adepts may have the ability to consciously leave their physical bodies while traveling in their Astral Bodies. The Astral Body or Astral Plane has various levels of evolution and is the heavenly abode where the soul resides after the disintegration of the physical body. The Astral Body is also known as the Body Double, the Desire Body, and the Emotional Body.

Atlantis: An ancient civilization of Earth, whose mythological genesis was the last Puranic Dvapara Yuga—the Bronze Age of the Yugas, and its demise occurred around the year 9628 BC. The legends of Atlantis claim the great empire co-existed with Ameru, Lemuria, and the Lands of Rama. According to Theosophical thought, Atlantis's evolving humanity brought about an evolutionary epoch of the Pink Ray on Earth, and the development of the Astral-Emotional bodies and the Heart Chakra. Ascended Master provenance claims the Els—now the Mighty Elohim of the Seven Rays—were the original Master Teachers to the spiritual seekers of Atlantis. Esoteric historians suggest three phases of political and geophysical boundaries best describe its ancient record: the Toltec Nation of Atlantis (Ameru); the Turian Nation of Atlantis (the invaders of the Land of Rama); and Poseid, the Island Nation of the present-day Atlantic Ocean. The early civilizations of Atlantis were ruled by the spiritually evolved Toltec and their spiritual teachings, ceremonies, and temples were dedicated to the worship of the sun. Atlantean culture later deteriorated into the use of nuclear weapons and cruelty towards other nations, including the use of genetic engineering. The demise of Atlantis was inevitable; however, modern-day geologists, archaeologists, and occultists all disagree to its factual timing. Ascended Master teachings affirm that Atlantis—a continent whose geophysical and political existence probably spanned well over 100,000 years—experienced several phases of traumatic Earth Change. This same belief is held by occult historians who allege Earth repeatedly cycles through periods of massive Earth Change and cataclysmic pole-shifts that activate tectonic plates which subsequently submerge whole continents and create vital new lands for Earth's successors.

Aura: The subtle energy field of luminous light that surrounds the human body.

Babajeran: A name for the Earth Mother that means, "Grandmother rejoicing."

Balance: "Put into proper order."

Blue Flame: The activity of the Blue Ray, based upon the activation of the individual will, manifests the qualities of truth, power, determination, and diligence in human endeavors. The Blue Flame is associated with the transformation of our individual choices, and its inherent processes align the individual will to the Divine Will through the HU-man qualities of detachment, steadiness, calm, harmony, and God-protection.

Blue Ray: A Ray is a perceptible light and sound frequency, and the Blue Ray not only resonates with the color blue, but is identified with the qualities of steadiness, calm, perseverance, transformation, harmony, diligence, determination, austerity, protection, humility, truthfulness, and self-negation. It forms one-third of the Unfed Flame within the heart—the Blue Ray of God Power, which nourishes the spiritual unfoldment of the human into the HU-man. Use of the Violet Flame evokes the Blue Ray into action throughout the light bodies, where the Blue Ray clarifies intentions and assists the alignment of the Will. In Ascended Master teachings the Blue Ray is alleged to have played a major role in the physical manifestation of the Earth's first Golden City—Shamballa and six of fifty-one Golden Cities emanate the Blue Ray's peaceful, yet piercing frequencies. The Blue Ray is esoterically linked to the planet Saturn, the development of the Will, the ancient Lemurian Civilization, the Archangel Michael, the Elohim Hercules, the Master Teacher El Morya, and the Eastern Doors of all Golden Cities.

Cause and effect: Every action causes an event, which is the consequence or result of the first. This law is often referred to as karma—or the sixth Hermetic Law.

Chakra(s): Sanskrit for wheel. Seven spinning wheels of human-bioenergy centers stacked from the base of the spine to the top of the head.

Chela: Disciple

Christ, the: The highest energy or frequency attainable on Earth. The Christ is a step-down transformer of the I AM energies, which enlighten, heal, and transform all human conditions of degradation and death.

Co-creation: Creating with the God-Source.

Collective Consciousness: The higher interactive structure of consciousness as two or more.

Compassion: Sensitivity and understanding for another's suffering and the desire to give aid to relieve human pain, distress, and anguish.

Consciousness: Awakening to one's own existence, sensations, and cognitions.

Decree: Statements of intent and power, similar to prayers and mantras, which are often integrated with the use of the I AM and requests to the I AM Presence.

Desire: Of the Source.

Divine Inheritor: Successor and progeny of the inner God-Source.

Divine Plan: The outcome of creative and Co-creative processes that provoke spiritual growth and evolution. From a traditional viewpoint, the will of God.

Divine Will: The idea of God's plan for humanity; however, from the perspective of the HU-man, the Divine Will is "choice."

Duality: An understanding that the world is divided into two perceptible categories.

Earth Changes: A prophesied Time of Change on the Earth, including geophysical, political, and social changes, alongside the opportunity for spiritual and personal transformation.

Earth's Grids: Geometrical patterns that cover the Earth and follow symmetrical links to sacred geometry and crystalline shapes.

Eastern Door: The East side of a Golden City gateway, also known as the Blue Door.

Eight-sided Cell of Perfection: An atomic cell located in the human heart. It is associated with all aspects of perfection, and contains and maintains a visceral connection with the Godhead.

Elemental: A nature being.

Elemental Kingdom: A kingdom comprising an invisible, subhuman group of creatures who act as counterparts to visible nature on Earth.

El Morya: Ascended Master of the Blue Ray, associated with the development of the will.

Emotional Body: A subtle body of light that exists alongside the physical body. It comprises desires, emotions, and feelings.

Energy Field: Distinct and definable layers of energy that exist around all forms of physical life: mineral, plant, animal, and human.

Energy-for-Energy: The transfer of energies. To understand this spiritual principle, one must remember Isaac Newton's Third Law of Motion: "for every action there is an equal and opposite reaction." However, while energies may be equal, their forms often vary. The Ascended Masters often use this phrase to remind chelas to properly compensate others to avoid karmic retribution, and repayment may take many different forms.

Fear Substance: Energy associated with threat, pain, and terror. According to Ascended Master Teachings, the fear substance is created through intense emotion, then physically absorbed and retained in the physical body after death. Plants, animals, and humans create the fear substance; however, plants do not retain this substance after harvest. This physical essence permeates all animal food products, especially meats after slaughter. The fear substance is considered to be addictive to evolving HU-mans, and is associated with spiritual devolution, decay, and destruction. The Violet Flame and dietary discipline is key to removing the fear substance from the human and evolving HU-man body.

Fifth Dimension: A spiritual dimension of cause, associated with thoughts, visions, and aspirations. This is the dimension of the Ascended Masters and the Archetypes of Evolution, the city of Shamballa, and the templates of all Golden Cities.

Fourth Dimension: A dimension of vibration associated with telepathy, psychic ability, and the dream world. This is the dimension of the Elemental Kingdom and the development of the super senses.

Gateway Adjutant Points: Two Golden City power points that are located on either side of each directional gateway of a Golden City Vortex and are situated to the outer perimeter of the Vortex.

Gobean: The first United States Golden City located in the states of Arizona and New Mexico. Its qualities are cooperation, harmony, and peace. Its Ray Force is blue, and its Master Teacher is El Morya.

Golden Age: A peaceful time on Earth prophesied to occur after the Time of Change. It is also prophesied that during this age human life spans are increased and sacred knowledge is revered. During this time the societies, cultures, and the governments of Earth reflect spiritual enlightenment through worldwide cooperation, compassion, charity, and love. Ascended Master teachings often refer to the Golden Age as the Golden-Crystal Age and the Age of Grace.

Golden Age of Kali Yuga: According to the classic Puranic timing of the Yugas, Earth is in a Kali-Yuga period that started around the year 3102

BCE the year that Krishna allegedly left the Earth. During this time period, which according to this Puranic timing lasts a total of 432,000 years—the ten-thousand year Golden Age period, also known as the Golden Age of Kali Yuga, is not in full force. Instead, it is a sub-cycle of higher light frequencies within an overall larger phase of less light energy.

This Golden Age is prophesied to raise the energy of Earth as additional light from the Galactic Center streams to our planet. This type of light is a non-visible, quasar-type light that is said to expand life spans and memory function, and nourish human consciousness, especially spiritual development. There are many theories as to when this prescient light energy began to flow to our planet. Some say it started about a thousand years ago, and others claim it began at the end of the nineteenth century. No doubt its influence has changed life on Earth for the better, and according to the I AM America Teachings, its effect began to encourage and guide human spiritual evolution around the year 2000 CE.

The Spiritual Teachers say that living in Golden Cities can magnify Galactic Energies and at their height, the energies will light the Earth between 45 to 48 percent—nearly reaching the light energies of a full-spectrum Treta Yuga or Silver Age on Earth. The Spiritual Teachers state, "The Golden Age is the period of time where harmony and peace shall be sustained."

Golden City Activation: A full comprehension of the word "activate" is key to understanding this spiritual phenomena. The following dictionary definitions describe its usage: "to make active;" "to make more active;" "to hasten reactions by various means"; and "to place in active status." So, the term Golden City Activation includes several meanings and applications to illustrate the four types of Golden City activations. (1) Ascended Master Activation: *Made Active.* The Spiritual Hierarchy first conceptualized the idea of the Golden Cities by the perfect out-picturing of these spiritual centers. Certain Master Teachers, Archangels, and Elohim—in cooperation with Mother Earth Babajeran—sponsor specific Golden Cities. Their task: to gather the energies of each divine municipality. The grid structure of Earth—in tandem with the focus of the appropriate Ray—is held in immaculate concept by each steward and coalesces the energies of each Golden City. And as consciousness increases, members of mankind seek its Fifth Dimension power as spiritual retreats. (2) Geophysical Activation: *More Active.* The interaction of Mother Earth and the Golden Cities—Fifth Dimensional structures—produces Third and Fourth Dimensional characteristics. This phenomenon creates a more active activation. The significance of Third Dimensional activation lies in its ability to generate a Vortex at the intersection of lei-lines. When eight of these invisible coordinates crisscross, a Vortex emerges, including the formation of Golden City Vortices. Vortices move in a clockwise/counterclockwise motion. Geophysically activated Golden Cities have a profound effect on humans: they experience longevity, greater healing abilities, and physical regeneration. In the

Fourth Dimension, Nature Kingdoms begin to interact with Vortex energies; human visitors experience telepathic and psychic abilities, and lucid dreaming. (3) Ceremonial Activation: *To Hasten Reactions by Various Means*. Ceremonial activations, inspired by humans who seek an intense result from a Golden City, occur on an emotional-astral level in areas throughout these sacred Vortices. Similar to pujas or yagyas—known in Hindu as sacrifices—fire or water-driven ceremonies neutralize difficult karmas and enhance beneficial human qualities. (4) Great Central Sun Activation: *To Place in Active Status*. Produced by a greater timing or origin, this type of activation relies on the energies that emanate from the Great Central Sun or Galactic Center. Some theosophical scholars say power from the Galactic Center sends subtle energies to our solar system via the planetary Fire Triplicity: Jupiter, Mars, and the Sun.

Golden City Doorway: The four gateways of the Golden City Vortex based on the cardinal directions of North, East, South, and West. They comprise the North Door (or the Black Door); the East Door (or the Blue Door); the South Door (or the Red Door); the West Door (or the Yellow Door). The center of a Golden City is known as the "Star" and is affiliated with the color white.

Golden City Grid: The matrix comprised of all Golden Cities covering the Earth.

Golden City Vortex: A Golden City Vortex—based on the Ascended Masters' I AM America material—are prophesied areas of safety and spiritual energies during the Times of Changes. Covering an expanse of land and air space, these sacred energy sites span more than 400 kilometers (270 miles) in diameter, with a vertical height of 400 kilometers (250 miles). Golden City Vortices, more importantly, reach beyond terrestrial significance and into the ethereal realm. This system of safe harbors acts as a group or universal mind within our galaxy, connecting information seamlessly and instantly with other beings. Fifty-one Golden City Vortices are stationed throughout the world, and each carries a different meaning, a combination of Ray Forces, and a Divine Purpose. A Golden City Vortex works on the principles of electromagnetism and geology. Vortices tend to appear near fault lines, possibly serving as conduits of inner-earth movement to terra firma. Golden Cities are symbolized by a Maltese Cross, whose sacred geometry determine their doorways, lei-lines, adjutant points, and coalescing Star energies. Since their energies intensify experiences with both the Fourth and Fifth Dimensions, Golden City Vortices play a vital role with the Ascension Process. The clockwise motion of the Vortex absorbs energy from its Ray Force, Ascended Master Hierarch, the Great Central Sun, and Mother Earth – Babajeran. Its counterclockwise motion releases energy. The spin of the Vortex creates a torsion field.

Gold(en) Ray: The Ray of Brotherhood, Cooperation, and Peace. The Gold Ray produces the qualities of perception, honesty, confidence, courage, and responsibility. It is also associated with leadership, independence, authority, ministration, and justice. The Gold Ray is currently influencing the spiritual growth and evolution of the divine HU-man. It is also associated with karmic justice and will instigate many changes throughout our planet including Earth Changes and social and economic change.

Golden Thread Axis: Also known as the Vertical Power Current. The Golden Thread Axis physically consists of the Medullar Shushumna, a life-giving nadi comprising one-third of the human Kundalini system. Two vital currents intertwine around the Golden Thread Axis: the lunar Ida Current, and the solar Pingala Current. According to the Master Teachers, the flow of the Golden Thread Axis begins with the I AM Presence, enters the Crown Chakra, and descends through the spinal system. It descends beyond the Base Chakra and travels to the core of the Earth. Esoteric scholars often refer to the axis as the Rod of Power, and it is symbolized by two spheres connected by an elongated rod. Ascended Master students and chelas frequently draw upon the energy of the Earth through the Golden Thread Axis for healing and renewal using meditation, visualization, and breath. *See Tube of Light*

Great Central Sun: The great sun of our galaxy, around which all of the galaxy's solar systems rotate. The Great Central Sun is also known as the Galactic Center, which is the origin of the Seven Rays of Light and Sound on Earth.

Great Purification: Primarily considered a Native American term, the Great Purification signals the end of one period of time for humanity and the beginning of a New Time.

Great Silence: The Master Teachings encourage a contemplative period of quiet and stillness to intensely apply spiritual energies in certain circumstances and situations. This period of tranquil power is often referred to as the Great Silence.

Great White Brotherhood and Sisterhood (Lodge): This fraternity of ascended and unascended men and women is dedicated to the universal uplifting of humanity. Its main objective includes the preservation of the lost spirit, and the teachings of the ancient religions and philosophies of the world. Its Mission: to reawaken the dormant ethical and spiritual spark among the masses. In addition to fulfilling spiritual aims, the Great White Lodge has pledged to protect mankind against the systematic assaults—which inhibit self-knowledge and personal growth—on individual and group freedoms.

Green Ray: The Ray of Active Intelligence is associated with education, thoughtfulness, communication, organization, the intellect, science, objectivity, and discrimination. It is also adaptable, rational, healing, and awakened. The Green Ray is affiliated with the planet Mercury.

Group Mind: A conscious intelligent force, formed by members of distinguished cultures, societal organizations, and more prominently by religious church members; the Group Mind is held together by the rituals and customs that are peculiar to its members; newcomers instantly sense the energies of the atmosphere, and will either accept or reject its influence. The physics of the Group Mind are important to comprehend, as this collective intelligence is purposely formed to aid the Aspirant to raise human consciousness beyond present limitations.

Guru: Another name for teacher.

Harmony: The first virtue of the Twelve Jurisdictions based on the principle of agreement.

Heart Chakra: Known in Sanskrit as the Anahata. The location is in the center of the chest. Its main aspect is Love and Relationships, and includes our ability to feel compassion, forgiveness, and hold our own Divine Purpose.

Hermetic Law: Philosophical beliefs and principles based on the writings of Hermes Trismegistus, the Greek sage who is analogous to the Egyptian God Thoth.

HU-man: The God-Man.

I AM: The presence of God.

I AM Presence: The individualized presence of God.

I AM THAT I AM: A term from Hebrew that translates to, "I Will Be What I Will Be." "I AM" is also derived from the Sanskrit Om (pronounced: A-U-M), whose three letters signify the three aspects of God as beginning, duration, and dissolution – Brahma, Vishnu, and Shiva. The AUM syllable is known as the omkara and translates to "I AM Existence," the name for God. "Soham," is yet another mystical Sanskrit name for God, which means "It is I," or "He is I." In Vedic philosophy, it is claimed that when a child cries, "Who am I?" the universe replies, "Soham – you are the same as I AM." The I AM teachings also use the name "Soham" in place of "I AM."

Initiation: Admission, especially into secret, advanced spiritual knowledge.

Immortality: Everlasting and deathless. Spiritual immortality embraces the idea of the eternal, unending existence of the soul. Physical immortality includes the notion of the timeless, deathless, and birthless body.

Inner Earth: Below the Earth's Crust lie many magnificent cities and cultures of various break-away races of humans, evolved HU-mans, and extraterrestrials. The Inner Earth is filled with reservoirs, streams, rivers, lakes, and oceans. According to metaphysical researchers the Earth is honey-combed with pervasive caves and subterranean caverns measuring hundreds of miles in diameter. This viewpoint is held by the Ascended Masters and shared throughout their Earth Changes Prophecies and historical narratives.

Judgment: The act of forming negative assumptions and critical opinions, primarily of fellow human beings.

Kali Yuga: The Age of Iron, or Age of Quarrel, when Earth receives twenty-five percent or less galactic light from the Great Central Sun.

Karma: Laws of Cause and Effect.

Kundalini: The coiled energy located at the base of the spine, often established in the lower Base and Sacral Chakras. In Sanskrit, Kundalini literally means coiled, and Kundalini Shatki (shatki means energy) is claimed to initiate spiritual development, wisdom, knowledge, and enlightenment.

Klehma: The fifth United States Golden City located primarily in the states of Colorado and Kansas. Its qualities are continuity, balance, and harmony; its Ray Force is White; and its Master Teacher is Serapis Bey.

Kuan Yin: The Bodhisattva of Compassion and teacher of Saint Germain. She is associated with all the Rays and the principle of femininity.

Kuthumi: An Ascended Master of the Pink, Ruby, and Gold Rays. He is a gentle and patient teacher who works closely with the Nature Kingdoms.

Law of Love: Perhaps every religion on Earth is founded upon the Law of Love, as the notion to "treat others as you would like to be treated." The Law of Love, however, from the Ascended Master tradition is simply understood as consciously living without fear, or inflicting fear on others. The Fourth of the Twelve Jurisdictions instructs Love is the Law of Allowing, Maintaining, and Sustainability. All of these precepts distinguishes love from an emotion or feeling, and observes Love as action, will, or choice. The Ascended Masters affirm, "If you live love, you will create love." This premise is fundamental to understand the esoteric underpinnings of the Law of Love. The Master Teachers declare that through practicing the Law of Love one experiences acceptance and understanding; tolerance, alongside detachment. Metaphysically, the Law of Love allows different and varied perceptions of ONE experience, situation, or circumstance to exist simultaneously. From this viewpoint the Law of Love is the practice of tolerance.

Law of Attraction and Repulsion: Like charges repel; unlike charges attract.

Lei-lines: Lines of energy that exist among geographical places, ancient monuments, megaliths, and strategic points. These energy lines contain electrical or magnetic points.

Light: "Love in action."

Light Body: A body of subtle energy surrounding the human body. It survives death, and develops and evolves over lifetimes. Also known as the aura, the light body divides into layers of light energy. These strata are referred to as light bodies or layers of the field of the aura.

Lords of Venus: A group of Ascended Masters who came to serve humanity. They once resided on the planet Venus.

Love: "Light in action." The fourth of the Twelve Jurisdictions evolves our understanding of love as the Law of Allowing, Maintaining, and Sustainability.

Malton: The second United States Golden City located in the states of Illinois and Indiana. Its qualities are fruition and attainment; its Ray Force is Gold and Ruby; and its Master Teacher is Kuthumi.

Mantra: Certain sounds, syllables, and sets of words that are deemed sacred. They often carry the ability to transmute karma, spiritually purify, and transform an individual.

Map of Rings: This Map depicts Earth covered with a worldwide grid of interlocking circles. The circles portray the elements of Earth: air, water, fire, and earth. Their interaction with one another results in the physical manifestation of Earth and her many alchemical and spiritual processes.

Master Teacher: A spiritual teacher from a specific lineage of teachers—gurus. The teacher transmits and emits the energy from that collective lineage.

Mastery: Possessing the consummate skill of command and self-realization over thought, feeling, and action.

Mental Body: A subtle light body of the Human Aura comprising thoughts.

Michael: The archangel of the Blue Ray. Archangel Michael is the protector of chelas and initiates of the Ascended Master tradition through the activity of the Blue Flame.

Monad: From an Ascended Master viewpoint, the Monad is the spark or flame of life of spiritual consciousness and it is also the Awakened Flame that is growing, evolving, and ultimately on the path to Ascension. Because of its presence of self-awareness and purpose, the Monad represents our dynamic will and the individualized presence of the Divine Father. Ultimately, the Monad is the spark of consciousness that is self-determining, spiritually awake, and drives the growth of human consciousness. The Monad is the indivisible, whole, divine life center of an evolving soul that is immortal and contains the momentum within itself to drive consciousness to learn, grow, and perfect itself in its evolutionary journey.

Northern Door: The North side of a Golden City gateway, also known as the Black Door.

Om Manaya Pitaya or Om Manaaya Patiya: This Ascended Master statement has several meanings. Two spiritual translations are: "I AM the Light of God" and "I AM the Seer of the Lord." The Sanskrit translation means: "Amen, honored Lord."

ONE: Indivisible, whole, harmonious Unity.

Oneness: A combination of two or more, which creates the whole

Mudra: A symbolic ceremonial or spiritual gesture, mostly expressed by the hands and fingers. It is often used by evolved spiritual beings and Ascended Masters to signify or emit spiritual energies.

Perception: Awareness and intuitive recognition.

Prophecy: A spiritual teaching given simultaneously with a warning. It's designed to change, alter, lessen, or mitigate the prophesied warning. This caveat may be literal or metaphoric; the outcome of these events are contingent on the choices and the consciousness of those willing to apply the teachings.

Purification: A clearing process, especially in spiritual practice, which frees consciousness from cumbersome or objectionable elements.

Rapture: A form of spiritual liberation, based on sincerity, peace, faith, and acceptance.

Ray: A force containing a purpose, which divides its efforts into two measurable and perceptible powers, light and sound.

Ruby Ray: The Ruby Ray is the energy of the Divine Masculine and Spiritual Warrior. It is associated with these qualities: energetic; passionate; devoted; determination; dutiful; dependable; direct; insightful; inventive; technical; skilled; forceful. This Ray Force is astrologically affiliated with the planet Mars and the Archangel Uriel, Lord Sananda, and Master Kuthumi. The Ruby Ray is often paired with the Gold Ray, which symbolizes Divine Father. The Ruby Ray is the evolutionary Ray Force of both the base and solar chakras of the HU-man; and the Gold and Ruby Rays step-down and radiate sublime energies into six Golden Cities.

Sacred Fire: The Unfed Flame of Divine Consciousness within the human heart. Often the term "Sacred Fire" is used to signify the Violet Fire.

Sacrifice: The spiritual ideal that through giving selflessly, or taking a short-term loss, that a greater long-term return for others is created.

Saint Germain: Ascended Master of the Seventh Ray, Saint Germain is known for his work with the Violet Flame of Mercy, Transmutation, Alchemy, and Forgiveness. He is the sponsor of the Americas and the I AM America material. Many other teachers and Masters affiliated with the Great White Brotherhood help his endeavors.

Sananda: The name used by Master Jesus in his ascended state of consciousness. Sananda means joy and bliss, and his teachings focus on revealing the savior and heavenly kingdom within.

Seamless Garment: The Ascended Masters wear garments without seams. This clothing is not tailored by hand but perfected through the thought and manifestation process.

Service: The fifth of Twelve Jurisdictions is a helpful act based upon the Law of Love.

Seven Rays: The traditional Seven Rays of Light and Sound are: the Blue Ray of Truth; the Yellow Ray of Wisdom; the Pink Ray of Love; the White Ray of Purity; the Green Ray of Healing; the Gold and Ruby Ray of Ministration; and the Violet Ray of Transmutation.

Shalahah: The fourth United States Golden City located primarily in the states of Montana and Idaho. Its qualities are abundance, prosperity, and healing; its Ray Force is Green; and its Master Teacher is Sananda.

Shaman: An intermediary between the natural world and the spirit world. Indigenous Shaman place a strong emphasis on their environments; nature spirits and animals play important roles and act as omens, messengers, and spirit guides.

Shamballa: Venusian volunteers, who arrived 900 years before their leader Sanat Kumara, built Earth's first Golden City. Known as the City of White, located in the present-day Gobi Desert, its purpose was to hold conscious light for Earth and to sustain her evolutionary place in the solar system.

Soul: The self-aware immortal essence unique to every living being

Southern Door: The South side of a Golden City gateway, also known as the Red Door.

Spiritual Hierarchy: A fellowship of Ascended Masters and their disciples. This group helps humanity function through the mental plane with meditation, decrees, and prayer. The term Spiritual Hierarchy often refers to the Great White Brotherhood and Sisterhood. However, the term also connotes the spiritual-social structure for the organization, its members, and the various states of member evolution. The hierarchy includes the different offices and activities that serve the Cosmic, Solar, Planetary, and Creative Hierarchies.

Spiritual Migration: The process of moving to and living in certain geophysical areas to purposely integrate and assimilate Earth's sacred energies for spiritual growth and evolution.

Star: The apex, or center of each Golden City.

Star seed: Souls and groups whose genetic origins are not from Earth. Many remain linked to one another from one lifetime to the next, as signified by the Atma Karaka, a Sanskrit term meaning "soul indicator." Star-seed consciousness is often referred to by the Spiritual Teachers as a family or soul group whose members have evolved to and share Fifth-Dimensional awareness. Star seeds can also contain members who have not yet evolved to this level, who are still incarnating on Earth.

Step-down Transformer: The processes instigated through the Cellular Awakening rapidly advance human light bodies. Synchronized with an Ascended Master's will, the awakened cells of light and love evolve the skills of a Step-Down Transformer to efficiently transmit and distribute currents of Ascended Master energy—referred to as an Ascended Master Current (A.M. Current). This metaphysical form of intentional inductive coupling creates an ethereal power grid that can be used for all types of healing.

Third Dimension: Thought, feeling, and action.

Third Eye: The inner eye, referring to the ajna (brow) chakra.

Thought, Feeling, and Action: In Ascended Master teachings and tradition, thought, feeling, and action are the cornerstones of the creation process. Thought represents the mental (causal) body and the Yellow Ray. Feeling represents the emotional (astral) body and the Pink Ray. Action represents the physical body and the Blue Ray.

Time of Change: The period of time currently underway. Tremendous changes in our society, cultures, and politics in tandem with individual and collective spiritual awakenings and transformations will abound. These events occur simultaneously with the possibilities of massive global warming, climactic changes, and seismic and volcanic activity—Earth Changes. The Time of Change guides the Earth to a New Time, the Golden Age.

Time of Testing: The Time of Testing is a period of seven to twenty years which began around the turn of the twenty-first century, following the time period known as the Time of Transition. According to Saint Germain and other Ascended Masters, the Time of Testing is perhaps one of the most turbulent periods mankind will experience and its first seven years is prophesied as a period of change and strife for many. As its title suggests, the Master Teachers claim this timeframe may challenge students by testing their spiritual acumen and inner strength.

Time of Transition: A twelve-year period when humanity experienced tremendous spiritual and intellectual growth, ushering in personal and global changes. In the year 2000 a new era, called the Time of Testing, got underway. It's a seven-year span of time when economies and societies encountered instability and insecurity. These years are also defined by the spiritual growth of humanity; Brotherly love and compassion play a key role in the development of the Earth's civilizations as mankind moves toward the Age of Cooperation.

True Memory: Memory, as defined by Ascended Master teachings, is not seen as a function of the brain, or the soul's recall of past events. Instead, True Memory is achieved through cultivating our perceptions and adjusting our individual perspective of a situation to the multiple juxtapositions of opinion and experience. This depth of understanding gives clarity and illumination to every experience. Our skill and Mastery through True Memory moves our consciousness beyond common experiences to individualized experiences whose perceptive power hones honesty and accountability. The innate truth obtained from many experiences through the interplay of multiple roles creates True Memory, and opens the detached and unconditional Law of Love to the chela.

Tube of Light: Light surges from the tributaries of the Human Energy System: Chakras, meridians, and nadis—to create a large pillar of light. Decrees, prayers, and meditation with the Tube of Light increase its force and ability to protect the individual's spiritual growth and evolution. *See Golden Thread Axis*

Twelve Jurisdictions: Twelve laws (virtues) for the New Times that guide consciousness to Co-create the Golden Age. They are Harmony, Abundance, Clarity, Love, Service, Illumination, Cooperation, Charity, Desire, Faith, Stillness, Creation/Creativity.

Unana: Unity Consciousness.

Unfed Flame: The Threefold Flame of divinity that exists in the heart and becomes larger as it evolves. The three flames represent Love (pink); Wisdom (yellow); and Power (blue).

Universal Laws: Laws that apply to the entire universe; considered a fundamental basis of nature and reality.

Vibration: The moving, swinging, or oscillation of energy. In Ascended Master teachings, vibration is associated with light's movement during physical and spiritual activities, as well as in the presence of the Masters.

Violet Flame: The Violet Flame is the practice of balancing karmas of the past through Transmutation, Forgiveness, and Mercy. The result is an opening of the Spiritual Heart and the development of bhakti—unconditional love and compassion. It came into existence when the Lords of Venus first transmitted the Violet Flame, also knows as Violet Fire, at the end of Lemuria to clear the Earth's etheric and psychic realms, and the lower physical atmosphere of negative forces and energies. This paved the way for the Atlanteans, who used it during religious ceremonies and as a visible marker of temples. The Violet Flame also induces Alchemy. Violet light emits the shortest wavelength and the highest frequency in the spectrum, so it induces a point of transition to the next octave of light.

Violet Flame Angels: Legions of Violet Flame Angels are claimed to carry the energies of the transmuting Violet Flame whenever they are called upon. The Angels of the Violet Flame protect the flame in its purity and dispense its transforming vibration.

Violet Ray: The Seventh Ray is primarily associated with Freedom and Ordered Service alongside Transmutation, Alchemy, Mercy, Compassion, and Forgiveness. It is served by the Archangel Zadkiel, the Elohim Arcturus, the Ascended Master Saint Germain and Goddess Portia.

Vortex: A Vortex is a polarized motion body that creates its own magnetic field, aligning molecular structures with phenomenal accuracy. Vortices are often formed where lei-lines (energy meridians of the Earth) cross. They are often called power spots as the natural electromagnetic field of the Earth is immensely strong in this type of location.

Wahanee: The third United States Golden City located primarily in the states of South Carolina and Georgia. Its qualities are justice, liberty, and freedom; its Ray Force is Violet; and its Master Teacher is Saint Germain.

White Ray: The Ray of the Divine Feminine is primarily associated with the planet Venus. It is affiliated with beauty, balance, purity, and cooperation. In the I AM America teachings the White Ray is served by the Archangel Gabriel and Archeia Hope; the Elohim Astrea and Claire; and the Ascended Masters Serapis Bey, Paul the Devoted, Reya, the Lady Masters Venus and Se Ray, and the Group of Twelve.

Will: Choice.

Write and Burn Technique: An esoteric technique venerated by Ascended Master students and chelas to transmute any unwanted situation or circumstance, primarily dysfunctional life patterns. This technique involves hand-writing and then burning a letter—a petition—to the I AM Presence for Healing and Divine Intervention.

Yuga: Large recurring periods of time employed in the Hindu timekeeping system.

Discography

This list provides the recording session date and name of the original selected recordings cited in this work that provide the basis for its original transcriptions.

Toye, Lori
Path of Light, I AM America Seventh Ray Publishing International Audiocassette. ℗ No.062900, 2000. © June 6, 2000.

Teachings on Vibration, I AM America Seventh Ray Publishing International, Audiocassette. ℗ No. 071300, 2000. © July 7, 2000.

Stars of the Golden Cities, I AM America Seventh Ray Publishing International, Audiocassette. ℗ No. 081700, © March 30, 2000.

Ascension of Consciousness, I AM America Seventh Ray Publishing International, Audiocassette. ℗ No. 090100, 2000. © September 1, 2000.

Temples of Consciousness, I AM America Seventh Ray Publishing International, Audiocassette. ℗ No. 101900, © October 10, 2000.

True Memory, I AM America Seventh Ray Publishing International, Audiocassette ℗ No. 110900, 2000. © November 9, 2000.

The Heart of Peace; Lighting the Heart of Peace, One, I AM America Seventh Ray Publishing International, Audiocassette ℗ No. 091600, 2000. © September 16, 2001.

Unified Plane of Understanding; Lighting the Heart of Peace, Two, I AM America Seventh Ray Publishing International, Audiocassette. ℗ No. 092000, © September 20, 2001.

Principles of Harmony, I AM America Seventh Ray Publishing International, Audiocassette. ℗ No. 101100, © October 10, 2001.

Science of Solution, I AM America Seventh Ray Publishing International, Audiocassette. ℗ No. 101800, © October 18, 2001.

Index

A

abundance 164
 definition 213
 through harmony 172
activation
 Golden City 38
addiction
 decree for the diet 46
 to fear 40
Adjutant Point
 definition 213
 of a Golden City 144
Africa
 Ancient Sahara 63
Akashic Record(s) 69
 and the I AM 79
 definition 213
 throughout Golden Cities 63
alchemy 55, 87
 and the Fourth Dimension 120
 and Wahanee 95
 definition 213
 in nature 158
Alchemy of Nature
 and the number five 158
alignment 171
 and affinity 69
 definition 213
animal behavior
 in humans 78
Animal Kingdom 52
animal products
 and diet 40
Archangel Michael
 and harmony 165
 definition 225
Archangel Michael's Blue Flame
 appendix and instruction 195
Archangels (the Seven)
 definition 213

"As above, so below."
 Golden City of Malton 57
Ascended Beings
 coming to Earth 141
Ascended Master(s) 147
 and the Golden Cities 89
 consciousness and metaphysics 122
 definition 115, 213
 leads through Universal Law 134
 service with Babajeran 141
Ascension 39, 65, 148, 162
 and Divine Love 77
 and Klehma 58, 97
 and overcoming animalistic behavior 80
 and perception 130
 and personal experience 74
 and review of karmic patterns 76
 and sponsorship through an Ascended Master 80
 and the Earth 116
 and the preparation of the physical body 118
 and unity consciousness 46
 as a "graduation of souls" 73
 definition 213
 Mass Ascensions 67
 multicultural 62
 spiral 59
Ascension Process
 definition 213
Ascension Valley(s) 67
 definition 214
Astral Body
 definition 214
 dominant Ray 47
astrology
 and Ray Forces 48
Atlantis 31
 definition 215
 Golden City of Malton 63
At-ONE-Ment 44, 58, 111
 definition 214
aura
 definition 215

awakening 113
  and consciousness 180
  divinity 187
Aztec and Incan culture
  Golden City of Klehma 64

B

Babajeran 88, 141
  and Prophecy 115
  and the inner kingdoms 124
  cooperation with the Ascended Masters 61
  definition 215
  Time of Change 126
balance 166
  definition 215
  The Cup of Balance 134
beliefs 161
Blue Flame 131
  decree 170
  definition 215
  invoking the Blue Flame for protection 195
Blue Ray
  and Gobean 57
  and harmony 166
  definition 216
  for transformation of karmic patterns 75
  restores balance 170
breath work
  and meditation in Stars 178
  and use of mudra 192
Bronze Age
  and consciousness 31
Brule Sioux Nation
  appendix 201

C

Candle Meditation
  appendix and instruction 197
  instructions 197
cause and effect
  definition 216

Celtic and Druid cultures
  Golden City of Malton 63
ceremonial work
  Golden City Star 142
chakra(s) 93, 158
  and Golden Cities 98
  definition 216
  function of Golden Cities 192
change 126
chaos
  before the balance of harmony 171
chela
  definition 216
  Master Teacher and light bodies 45
choice 92, 102, 113, 134
  and the Temple of Gobean 94
Christ Consciousness 30, 134, 152, 183
Christ Plane 149, 152
Christ, the
  and the ONE 184
  definition 216
clairaudience 123
Co-creation 88, 94
  and groups of seven 154
  definition 216
Collective Consciousness 88
  and Earth Changes 89
  definition 216
  Golden City 66
  manipulation by the media 92
  "Where we go ONE, we go ALL." 67
compassion 112, 135, 163
  and the Law of Love 73
  definition 216
  heals the emotional body 50
conscious immortality 126
  "Life exists beyond what is seen." 119

consciousness 66, 150, 181
  and Ascension 81
  and awakening 180
  and diet 32
  and mind 40
  and perception 172
  and problems 183
  and the I AM Presence 110
  and the Master Teacher 44
  and the ONE 36
  collective 72
  definition 216
  expansion 171
  five initiations 97
  Golden City Grid 61
  group 142
  higher states 188
  Temples of Consciousness 143
consciousness shift
  and diet 51
crisis
  moving through 182
Crown Chakra 98
Cup of Balance 180

D

darkness 29
death
  losing loved ones 151
decree
  definition 217
  for compassion 136
  for harmony 166
  for our world leaders 136
  for perfection 29
  for the Blue Flame of Harmony 170
  for the Divine Plan 132
  for the Divine Will 92
  for Tube of Light 42
  for Violet Ray 55
  groups of seven 153
  Stars of Golden City Vortices 154
  to balance dual forces 149
  to break addiction to animal products 46

  to call Ray Forces into activity 48
  to command the Unfed Flame 91
  to remove problems 185
  to transmute genetic fear 34
  two or more are joined 153
desire 50
  definition 217
detachment 87, 103, 107
  and spiritual evolution 74
diet
  and vibration 32
  Ascension and the emotional body 81
  assimilation of light and sound 41
  changes your relationship to Earth 51
  decree to break addiction 46
  for entering the Golden City Star 63
  guidelines 40
  vegetable and the maturation process 42
discipline
  and diet 40
  and the Master Teacher 109
disease
  and harmony 164
  vibration and healing 188
Divine Cell
  Eight-sided Cell of Perfection 125
Divine Inheritance
  and the I AM Presence 35
Divine Inheritor
  definition 217
Divine Intervention
  Golden City Grid 61
Divine Love 82
  beyond illusion 76
Divine Mother 141
Divine Plan 35, 131, 150
  definition 217
Divine Will 131
  and the mental body 78
  definition 217
"Down with death. Conscious immortality arise!" 105
dream space
  and the Master Teacher 45

duality 29, 35, 133
  and the Law of Attraction 148
  definition 217

E

Earth
  and diet 51
  and healing through humanity's collective mind 192
  as a schoolroom 72
  secret chambers 32
Earth Changes 62, 99, 141
  and collective consciousness 89
  and emotional energy 191
  and purification 124
  and the Fourth Dimension 120
  definition 217
  global warming 59
  leap in consciousness 117
  protection in the Stars 155
Earth's Grid
  a new vibration 142
Earth's Grids
  definition 217
Earth's Poles
  and the Violet Flame 37
Eastern Doors 69, 156
  definition 217
ego 36
Egypt
  Golden City of Gobean 63
Eight-sided Cell of Perfection 90, 93, 140, 169
  connects to the dimensions 125
  definition 217
  "Demonstrates the truth." 129
  entering timelessness 44
elemental
  definition 217
Elemental Kingdom
  and Malton 95
  and the Fourth Dimension 119
  definition 217
  keeps the Earth in perfected order 126

Elemental Life Force 124
  and the Fourth Dimension 123
El Morya 50, 72, 140, 160
  and Gobean 94
  and harmony 165
  appendix 197
  definition 217
  meditation technique 44
emotional body 49
  and diet 81
  and karmic patterns 85
  and money 84
  definition 217
  healing through compassion 50
emotional energy
  and the Earth Plane 191
emotion(s) 77, 102
  and physical activity 84
  and the Plant Kingdom 41
energy
  building 168
energy field
  definition 217
energy field(s)
  and balance 171
  calmed through harmony 165
energy-for-energy 85
  and the Master Teacher 46
  definition 218
experience
  and spiritual expansion 106
  and the soul's education 78

F

fear 30, 132
  and ego 36
  choice and love 104
  genetic 33
  moving out of 179
  the presence of the Ascended Masters 147
  when you are hindered by fear 140

fear substance
  and diet 41
  and the Plant Kingdom 41
  definition 218
field of action 30
Fifth Dimension 158
  and Golden Cities 89
  and Wahanee 95
  chakras 99
  definition 218
  harmonic of twenty-eight 121
five
  symbology 158
five senses
  limitation and expansion 128
Five Teachings of Spiritual Acceleration 58
Flame of Divinity 27
Flame of Freedom 61
Flame of Light
  and the Candle Meditation 197
flesh eating
  and consciousness 32
  and vibration 40
force field
  harmony 168
forgiveness
  and natural law 112
  of self 113
fountain of youth 111
Fourth Dimension 118, 189
  and Golden Cities 89
  and Golden City energies 119
  and the Time of Change 126
  chakras 99
  definition 218
  harmonic of fourteen 121
  opens through the heart 116
freedom 159
  the divine birthright 113
  through restriction 82

G

Gateway Adjutant Points
  definition 218
  Golden City Vortex 143
genetic codes 104
  and perfection 91
  and the Eight-sided Cell of Perfection 97
genetic fear 33
  decree to transmute 34
genetic manipulation 32, 90
  reversal through the Violet Flame 97
genetics
  and animalistic behavior 78, 82
  and memory 108
global warming 66, 172
Gobean
  definition 218
Gobean Mystery School
  and harmony 164
  Egypt 63
God I AM 103, 140, 160
  and applying the will 186
Golden Age 141, 155, 189
  definition 218
  of Kali Yuga 91
Golden Age of Kali Yuga
  definition 218
Golden Cities and Chakras
  appendix and instruction 203
Golden City Activation
  definition 219
Golden City Doorway
  appendix and illustration 205
  definition 220
Golden City Grid
  definition 220
Golden City of
  Gobean 38, 57, 94, 164
    definition 218
  Klehma 96
    definition 223
  Malton 57, 95
    definition 224

Shalahah 58, 96
　definition 227
Wahanee 57, 95
　definition 230
Golden City Vortex
　activation 38
　and Akashic Records 63
　and chakras 98
　and Elemental Life Force 125
　and healing 93
　and Ray Forces 37
　and spiritual initiation 66
　and spiritual practice 156
　and the Fourth Dimension 119
　and their function 192
　and the Master Teacher 45
　definition 220
　Doorways 56, 69
　five teachings 58
　future population 100
　gateway points 143
　great schools 63
　Grid 56, 61, 64
　moving to 47
　serve the physical aspect of the Ascension 117
　spending time in 99
　spiritual function 88
　Star 56, 58, 142, 154
　temples 143
　"timing and intention" 123
　traveling to 145
Golden Thread Axis
　definition 221
Gold Ray
　definition 221
gourd of ashes 201
Great Central Sun 56
　and greater light 190
　and the Golden Cities 89
　and the pathway of sound frequencies 127
　and the two solar suns 190
　and the Violet Ray 33
　definition 221

divine timing 141
Ray Forces 61
Great I AM 181
Great Purification
　appendix 201
　definition 201, 221
　"Knows no boundaries." 61
　spiritual growth 60
Great Silence 134, 138
　definition 221
Great White Brotherhood 29
　messengers and beliefs 161
　new Master Teachers 159
　protection 154
Great White Brotherhood and Sisterhood
　definition 221
Green Ray 179
　and Shalahah 58
　and the White Ray 67
　definition 222
group consciousness 142
Group Mind
　and harmony 174
　definition 222
guru
　definition 222
guru and chela relationship 80

H

harmony 150, 155
　and its influence on Collective Consciousness 72
　and relocation 66
　and the group 174
　decree 166
　definition 222
　Principle of Harmony 163
　"Harmony lets all flow." 167
Hawkins, Dr. David 208

healing
  and consciousness 188
  and the Violet Flame 37
  Earth 192
  through the Master within 180
heart
  and Earth Changes 66
  entering the Golden City Star 62
  lessons of the heart 123
  opens Fourth Dimension 116
Heart Chakra 98
  and harmony 167
  definition 222
Heart of Compassion 179
Hermetic Law 35, 132
  definition 222
higher mind
  identifying emotions 84
Hopi Prophecies 201
HU-man 107
  definition 222
  developing through the Candle Meditation 197
human aura
  Ascension 39
  definition 215
  Fourth Dimension 122
humanity's history
  Akashic Records 63
human senses
  and seven harmonics 122

I

I AM
  and the spiritual awakening 79
  and the will 92
  and Unana 150
  definition 222
  remembering 111
I AM America
  dispensation through the Rays 71
I AM America Map
  use of mudra 191
I AM America Prophecies
  Earth Changes events 60
I AM Presence 35, 60, 181
  and the Tube of Light 42
  and the Unfed Flame 91
  call for harmony 166
  definition 222
  Golden City Star 63
  perfected state 180
  releases the energy of the Great I AM 180
I AM THAT I AM 44
  and Divine Order 78
  definition 222
illusion 28, 76, 148
  and the dark side 29
  release from 33
immortal
  connection with a Master Teacher 45
immortality 101
  definition 223
  of consciousness 118
India
  Golden City of Shalahah 64
initiation 59
  definition 223
  through the Golden Cities 99
Inner Earth
  and the Violet Flame 37
  and the Violet Ray 31
  definition 223
  secret chambers 32
intention 73, 123, 148, 166
  and money 84

J

Jacob's Ladder 62
joy
  and camaraderie along the path 182
judgment
  and surrender 104
  and the emotional body 85
  definition 223
  of self 28
  self-created hells 60

K

Kali Yuga 125
  and the Golden Age 90
  definition 223
karma 30, 75, 162
  and the use of the Violet Flame 175
  and the Violet Flame 132
  definition 223
karmic patterns 75
Klehma
  definition 223
"Knowledge is not for the un-initiate." 152
Kuan Yin 211
  definition 223
Kundalini 94
  definition 223
Kuthumi
  definition 223

L

Law of Attraction 50, 135, 137, 148, 156
  and harmony 173
  and peace 193
  Write and Burn Technique 199
Law of Attraction and Repulsion
  definition 224
Law of Love 96, 111
  and freedom 105
  and the Violet Ray 33
  definition 223

Law(s) of
  Abundance and Prosperity 66
  Compassion
    and higher consciousness 73
  Cooperation 58
  Harmony 66
  Love 73
  Momentum 55
  ONE 67
  Opposites 164
  Rhythm 132
  Unity 51
lei-line(s) 64, 88, 140, 191, 192
  and the Seven Temples 32
  definition 224
  Golden City 56
lessons 28
light
  definition 224
Light and Sound
  and the physical body 41
  Ascension 39
  leap in the Fourth and Fifth Dimensions 121
light body (bodies)
  and the Master Teacher 45
  definition 224
Light of God 30
loneliness
  "You are never alone." 33
Lords of Karma
  and intervention through the Violet Flame 175
Lords of Venus 31
  and the Violet Ray 32
  definition 224
love 53, 73, 107
  and detachment 108
  and the path of the heart 181
  definition 224
  expression as compassion 50
  Heart of Love 187
  "Will move a mountain." 129

M

Malton
  definition 224
Malton Mystery School
  Atlantis 63
mantra(s)
  and the Violet Ray 32
  definition 224
Map of Rings 64
  definition 224
Master
  within 134, 180, 181, 187
Master Kuthumi
  and Malton 95
"Master lies within." 161
Master Teacher(s) 157
  and discipline 109
  and energy for energy 85
  and Star seeds 65
  and the "gates of freedom" 130
  and the Star energies 59
  appearance 59
  assists the student 49
  connection with 43
  definition 225
  gateway points 143
  prepares the consciousness 44
  preparing for the Master through the Violet Flame 50
  seven year timeframe 45
  vibration suited to the student 50
  write and burn technique 47
Mastery 149
  and harmony 170
  and states of consciousness 182
  definition 225
  thoughts, feelings, actions 45
media
  manipulation of Collective Consciousness 92

meditation 51, 165, 177
  El Morya's technique 44
  for Mother Earth 192
  in Golden City Doorways 157
  Sananda's teachings 153
memory 102
  and choice 106
  and perception 103
  bondage through 104
  the developed memory 112
Mental Body
  and Divine Love 83
  and karmic patterns 75
  definition 225
Michael
  definition 225
mind 102
  and the Ascension 76
  "Builder of consciousness." 40
mirror(s) 36
Monad 151
  definition 225
money
  and emotional experiences 84
Mother Earth 68
  and balance 171
mudra
  definition 225
  for Sananda's meditation 178
  Golden City Star 191
music
  energy of harmony 170
Mystery School of Klehma
  Pleiades 64

N

natural selection 108
nature
  and Malton 57
neutrality 164
New Times 189
  and group harmony 174
  and harmony 164
  and new way of being 176

Northern Doors 69, 156
 definition 225

O

octave
 metaphysical barrier 122
Om Manaya Pitaya
 definition 225
"Om Sheahah. I AM as ONE" 58, 96
ONE 29, 107
 and Ascension 80
 and harmony 167
 and oversoul 110
 and the Candle Meditation 197
 and the detachment of memories 103
 and the I AM Presence 180
 and the Violet Ray 35
 definition 225
 white and gold 139
Oneness
 and harmony 165
 as the fountain of youth 111
 definition 225
openness
 and awakening 187
optimism 186
out-picturing 78
oversoul 109
ozone layer 172

P

pain
 forgetting 74
pairs of opposites 151
peace 137, 142
 and meditation 192
perception 151
 and age 102
 and the dimensions 128
 definition 225
 leverages consciousness 172

perfection 29
 and genetics 91
 and the Ascension 117
 and the Eyes of God 180
physical activity
 discharges emotion 84
physical body
 and the Ascension 116
Plant Kingdom
 and diet 41
Pleiades
 Golden City of Klehma 64
Pluto 190
polarity 34
 births neutrality 184
polarization
 and fear 133
population
 future centers Golden Cities 100
Principle of Cooperation 167
Principle of Harmony 163
problems
 and solutions are ONE 183
 choice and solutions 185
 remove through Violet Flame 185
Prophecy 88, 100, 133, 148
 and Babajeran 115
 and positive energy 186
 and the Green Ray 71
 definition 225
purification
 and the Earth Changes 124
 definition 226

R

Rapture 62, 116
 definition 226
 Mass Ascension 67
rate of spin
 vibration and Ascension 39
Ray Force(s) 141
 and Golden Cities 37
 and harmony 166
 and individualization 143
 and the Fourth and Fifth Dimensions 127
 and the Golden Cities 38
 arcing into Golden City 56
 balancing 48
 entering the Golden City Star 62
 Golden Cities 157
 Golden City and Ascended Master 89
 integration with the I AM Presence 42
 Master Teacher 59
 Stars 69
Ray(s)
 and the ONE 174
 Astral Body 42
 definition 226
 dominant Ray of Astral Body 47
relocation
 and harmony 66
restriction and freedom 82
Root Chakra 98
Ruby and Gold Ray 57
Ruby Ray
 definition 226

S

Sacred Fire 60, 95
 and the Oneship 44
 definition 226
sacred geometry 95

sacrifice 27, 66
 and diet 51
 and the ego 36
 definition 226
 energy for energy 46
Saint Germain
 and the Violet Flame 211
 builds an energy force field 168
 definition 226
Sananda 62, 74, 154, 207
 and Shalahah 96
 definition 226
 Inner Garden 58
 meditation and teaching 139
 meditation technique 177
 "Om Sheahah" 36
 Sunday Peace Meditation 207
 teachings on collective energy body 178
 the open door 108
 "The time has come for man to receive the gift." 116
Seamless Garment 28, 30, 93, 102
 definition 226
secret chamber(s) 32
security and emotion 85
self-examination 149
self-judgment 28, 33
separation
 and the Divine Plan 35
service
 definition 226
 releases karma 175
Seven Rays
 definition 227
Seven Temples of the Violet Ray 32
Seventh Seal 158
Sexual Chakra 98
Shalahah
 definition 227
Shalahah Mystery School
 Ancient India 64
shaman
 definition 227

Shamballa
  City of White 64
  definition 227
Silver Age
  and consciousness 31
Singh, Major Kulwant 207
Sioux Prophecies 201
Six Map Scenario
  teaching of choice and will 92
Solar Plexus Chakra 98
solutions
  and empowerment 188
  and problems exists as ONE 183
soul 28, 111
  definition 227
sound
  and the Great Central Sun 127
Southern Doors 69, 156
spirit guides 65
Spiritual Acceleration
  five teachings 58
  in the Golden City Stars 62
spiritual evolution
  through the Golden Cities 144
spiritual growth
  through the Earth Changes 60
Spiritual Hierarchy
  definition 227
  work with Babajeran 88
spiritual initiation
  and Gobean 94
spiritual migration 58
Spiritual Migration
  definition 227
spiritual refinement
  through a Master Teacher 51
spiritual unfolding 27
spoken word 92
Star of Klehma 68

Star(s) 69
  and interconnectivity 68
  and meditation 177
  and spiritual practice 155
  balance Earth's turmoil 191
  critical points 208
  definition 227
  energies coalesce 156
  entering the Golden City Star 62
  heigth 154
  of the Golden City 58, 88
  the Golden City Star 142
  United States cities and towns 208
Star seed(s) 61
  and animalistic behavior 82
  definition 227
  genetic lineage 65
Step-down Transformer
  and the I AM Presence 42
  definition 228
Sun
  the two Suns 190
Sunday Peace Meditation
  appendix and instruction 207
  for violence 191
super storms 66
sympathetic harmony 50
sympathetic resonance 35

T

teamwork 172
  and harmony 166
Temple Divine 159
Temple of Mercy 211
tests 160
Third Dimension
  and limitation 128
  definition 228
  harmonic of seven 121
Third Eye Chakra 98
thought
  and transforming for Ascension 76

thought, feeling, and action 88, 173
  definition 228
Three Standards
  appendix and instruction 195
  refinement through the Violet Flame 43
Throat Chakra 98
time
  and the perception of aging 102
  experience and perception 105
timelessness
  and the Eight-sided Cell of Perfection 44
Time of Ascension
  "We become unbound by the physical." 117
Time of Change 149
  definition 228
  humanity and Babajeran 126
Time of Testing 101, 132, 182
  definition 228
Time of Transition 159
  and Prophecy 133
  definition 228
"To do, to dare, and to be silent." 79
tolerance 112, 162
transmute energy patterns
  Write and Burn Technique 199
trinity 30
Trivedi, Prashant 202
True Memory 74
  definition 229
  vibrates the God-man 105
true self
  remembrance of 110
Tube of Light 51, 132, 195
  appendix and instruction 195
  application of 42
  definition 229
twelve
  sacred number 189
twelve avatars 189

Twelve Jurisdictions 163, 167, 189
  and aboundance 165
  definition 229
"Two become as ONE." 169, 171

U

Unana 29, 150, 158, 169, 178
  and Christ Consciousness 135, 183
  and the White Ray 67
  definition 229
  Sunday Peace Meditation 207
Unfed Flame 27, 93, 97
  decree to command 91
  definition 229
  genetic manipulation 90
unified body of light
  transmutes the physical body 118
United States
  working towards harmony 173
Unity Consciousness 46, 68, 80, 96
  unified field of human consciousness 207
Universal Law
  and the Ascended Master 134
  definition 229
unseen energy
  and the chela 49

V

vibration
  and diet 40
  and the Animal Kingdom 52
  animal free diet 63
  definition 229
  of the Master Teacher 50
  sympathetic harmony 52
victim
  no longer 179
Violet Flame 52, 83, 106, 147, 163
  and compassion 113
  and harmony 164
  and healing 170
  and karma 175
  and obstructions 101

appendix and instruction 195
calling forth the consuming fire 195
Chakra System 154
changing attitude and perception 186
decree for the dimensions 130
decree to light compassion 136
definition 229
for suffering 152
for the Blue Flame of Harmony 170
for the will 132
for world leadership 136
invocation at sunrise, sunset 212
overcomes Kali Yuga 125
preparation to meet the Master Teacher 50
prior to meditation 153
purification of the room 153
refinement of 43
Spiritual Lineage 211
the great liberator 113
to balance duality 149
to remove problems 185
with the Tube of Light 42
Violet Flame Angels
definition 230
write and burn technique 47
Violet Flame Decree
for attacks and threats 36
for genetic fear 34
for the Golden City Journey 70
to break addiction to animal products in diet 46
Violet Ray 28, 30, 55, 60
and emotional responses 84
and Saint Germain 87
and the Ascension 75
and the Green Ray 67
and the Law of Love 33
and the Lords of Venus 31
and the secret chambers 32
and the Seven Temples 32
and Wahanee 57
and write and burn techniques 84
combines all mantras 32
definition 230

emanation process 33
to quiet the mind 76
use to overcome attachments 84
Violet Ray Decree
for perfection 29
volcanic eruptions
grid activations 64
Vortex
as a chakra 93
definition 230

W

Wahanee
definition 230
Wahanee Mystery School
Africa 63
Western Doors 69, 156
"What is poison for one is bread for another." 162
"When one door closes, another then opens." 176
White Ray 96
and healing for Ascension 73
and Klehma 58
definition 230
will 92
alignment 57
and God I AM 186
assistance by the Master Teacher 49
decree for the Divine Will 92
definition 230
world leaders
decree for 136
World Trade Center 137
Write and Burn Technique 84, 199
appendix and instruction 199
definition 230
for contact with a Master Teacher 47

Y

yuga 31
definition 230

About Lori and Lenard Toye

Lori Toye is not a Prophet of doom and gloom. The fact that she became a Prophet at all is highly unlikely. Reared in a small Idaho farming community as a member of the conservative Missouri Synod Lutheran church, Lori had never heard of meditation, spiritual development, reincarnation, channeling, or clairvoyant sight.

Her unusual spiritual journey began in Washington State, when, as advertising manager of a weekly newspaper, she answered a request to pick up an ad for a local health food store. As she entered, a woman at the counter pointed a finger at her and said, "You have work to do for Master Saint Germain!"

The next several years were filled with spiritual enlightenment that introduced Lori, then only twenty-two years old, to the most exceptional and inspirational information she had ever encountered. Lori became a student of Ascended Master teachings.

Awakened one night by the luminous figure of Saint Germain at the foot of her bed, her work had begun. Later in the same year, an image of a map appeared in her dream. Four teachers clad in white robes were present, pointing out Earth Changes that would shape the future United States.

Five years later, faced with the stress of a painful divorce and rebuilding her life as a single mother, Lori attended spiritual meditation classes. While there, she shared her experience, and encouraged by friends, she began to explore the dream through daily meditation. The four Beings appeared again, and expressed a willingness to share the information. Over a six-month period, they gave over eighty sessions of material, including detailed information that would later become the I AM America Map.

Clearly she had to produce the map. The only means to finance it was to sell her house. She put her home up for sale, and in a depressed market, it sold the first day at full asking price.

She produced the map in 1989, rolled copies of them on her kitchen table, and sold them through word-of-mouth. She then launched a lecture tour of the Northwest and California. Hers was the first Earth Changes Map published, and many others have followed, but the rest is history.

From the tabloids to the *New York Times*, *The Washington Post*, television interviews in the U.S., London, and Europe, Lori's Mission was to honor the material she had received. The material is not hers, she stresses. It belongs to the Masters, and their loving, healing approach is disseminated through the I AM America Publishing Company operated by her husband and spiritual partner, Lenard Toye.

Lenard Toye, originally from Philadelphia, PA, was born into a family of professional contractors and builders, and has a remarkable singing voice. Lenard's compelling tenor voice replaced many of the greats at a moment's notice—Pavarotti and Domingo, including many performances throughout Europe. When he retired from music, he joined his family's business yet pursued his personal interests in alternative healing.

He attended *Barbara Brennan's School of Healing* to further develop the gift of auric vision. Working together with his wife Lori, they organized free classes of healing techniques and the channeled teachings. Their instructional pursuits led them to form the *School of the Four Pillars* which includes holistic and energy healing and Ascended Master Teachings. In 1995 and 1996 they sponsored the first Prophecy Conferences in Philadelphia and Phoenix, Arizona. His management and sales background has played a very important role in his partnership with his wife Lori and their publishing company. Other publications include three additional Prophecy maps, thirteen books, a video, and more than sixty audio tapes based on sessions with Master Teacher Saint Germain and other Ascended Masters.

Spiritual in nature, I AM America is not a church, religion, sect, or cult. There is no interest or intent in amassing followers or engaging in any activity other than what Lori and Lenard can do on their own to publicize the materials they have been entrusted with.

They have also been directed to build the first Golden City community. A very positive aspect of the vision is that all the maps include areas called, "Golden Cities." These places hold a high spiritual energy, and are where sustainable communities are to be built using solar energy alongside classical feng shui engineering and infrastructure. The first community, Wenima Village, is currently being planned for development.

Concerned that some might misinterpret the Maps' messages as doom and gloom and miss the metaphor for personal change, or not consider the spiritual teachings attached to the maps, Lori emphasizes that the Masters stressed that this was a Prophecy of choice. Prophecy allows for choice in making informed decisions and promotes the opportunity for cooperation and harmony. Lenard and Lori's vision for I AM America is to share the Ascended Masters' prophecies as spiritual warnings to heal and renew our lives.

Books and Maps by Lori Toye

Books:

NEW WORLD WISDOM SERIES: *Book One, Two, and Three*

FREEDOM STAR: *Prophecies that Heal Earth*

THE EVER PRESENT NOW: *A New Understanding of Consciousness and Prophecy*

I AM AMERICA ATLAS: *Based on the Maps, Prophecies, and Teachings of the Ascended Masters*

GOLDEN CITY SERIES
  Book One: Points of Perception
  Book Two: Light of Awakening
  Book Three: Divine Destiny
  Book Four: Sacred Energies of the Golden Cities
  Book Five: Temples of Consciousness

I AM AMERICA TRILOGY
  Book One: A Teacher Appears
  Book Two: Sisters of the Flame
  Book Three: Fields of Light

I AM AMERICA COLLECTION
  Building the Seamless Garment: Revealing the Secret Teachings of Ascension and the Golden Cities

Maps:
  I AM America Map
  Freedom Star World Map
  United States 6-Map Scenario
  United States Golden City Map

I AM AMERICA PUBLISHING & DISTRIBUTING
P.O. Box 2511, Payson, Arizona, 85547, USA. (928) 978-6435
I AM America Online Bookstore:
www.iamamerica.com
For More Information:
www.loritoye.com

About I AM America

I AM America is an educational and publishing foundation dedicated to disseminating the Ascended Masters' message of Earth Changes Prophecy and Spiritual Teachings for self-development. Our office is run by the husband and wife team of Lenard and Lori Toye who hand-roll maps, package, and mail information and products with a small staff. Our first publication was the I AM America Map, which was published in September 1989. Since then we have published three more Prophecy maps, thirteen books, and numerous recordings based on the channeled sessions with the Spiritual Teachers.

We are not a church, a religion, a sect, or cult and are not interested in amassing followers or members. Nor do we have any affiliation with a church, religion, political group, or government of any kind. We are not a college or university, research facility, or a mystery school. El Morya told us that the best way to see ourselves is as, "Cosmic Beings, having a human experience."

In 1994, we asked Saint Germain, "How do you see our work at I AM America?" and he answered, "I AM America is to be a clearinghouse for the new humanity." Grabbing a dictionary, we quickly learned that the term "clearinghouse" refers to "an organization or unit within an organization that functions as a central agency for collecting, organizing, storing, and disseminating documents, usually within a specific academic discipline or field." So inarguably, we are this too. But in uncomplicated terms, we publish and share spiritually transformational information because at I AM America there is no doubt that, "A Change of Heart can Change the World."

With Violet Flame Blessings,
Lori & Lenard Toye

For more information or to visit our online bookstore, go to:
www.iamamerica.com
www.loritoye.com

To receive a catalog by mail, please write to:
I AM America
P.O. Box 2511
Payson, AZ 85547

Awaken to the Change Within

FROM THE BESTSELLING AUTHOR OF THE I AM AMERICA MAPS

The Ever Present Now

A NEW UNDERSTANDING OF CONSCIOUSNESS AND PROPHECY

LORI ADAILE TOYE

The Ever Present Now
ISBN: 9781880050507

loritoye.com
iamamerica.com

Or, call 928-978-6435
or Amazon.com

I AM America Trilogy
The contemporary Spiritual Journey

A Teacher Appears	Sisters of the Flame	Fields of Light
ISBN: 9781800050446	ISBN: 9781800050262	ISBN: 9781800050613
254 pages	216 pages	310 pages

This series of insightful books, written by the creator of the acclaimed *I AM America Maps* shares a fresh and personal viewpoint of the contemporary spiritual journey. Lori Toye was just twenty-two years old when she first encountered Ascended Master teaching. The *I AM America Trilogy* takes us back to the beginning of her experiences with her spiritual teachers and includes insights that have never been disclosed in any previous books or writings. In "A Teacher Appears," learn how true wisdom and the inner teacher is within all of us. "Sisters of the Flame," continues an initiatory passage into the feminine with the Cellular Awakening. "Fields of Light," explains how to integrate and Master our spiritual light through soul-transcending teachings of Ascension. Lori's personal story is interwoven throughout the *I AM America Trilogy* in a rich tapestry of spiritual techniques, universal wisdom, and knowledge gained through a life-changing spiritual journey.

I AM America Atlas

Updated Edition!
Contains all of the
I AM America Maps
Full color
Over 100 Maps
164 pages

New World Wisdom Series

Spiritual Teachings from
the Ascended Masters
Books One, Two, and Three

Spiritual Teaching for the New Times

For more information:
loritoye.com
iamamerica.com
or call (928) 978-6435

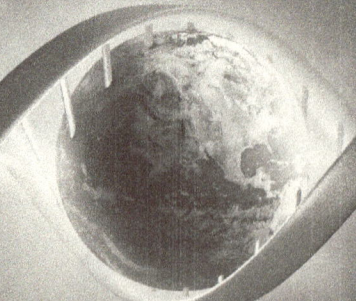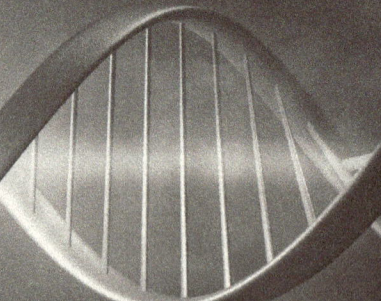

Printed in the USA
CPSIA information can be obtained
at www.ICGtesting.com
CBHW031258191024
16128CB00002BA/33